MARCO 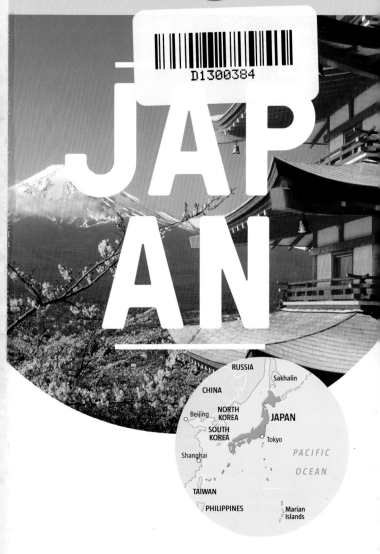 POLO

D1300384

JAP AN

APR 2 3 2018

RUSSIA
Sakhalin
CHINA
NORTH
KOREA
Beijing
JAPAN
SOUTH
KOREA
Tokyo
PACIFIC
Shanghai
OCEAN
TAIWAN
PHILIPPINES
Marian
Islands

www.marco-polo.com

FREE!

THE TOURING APP

shows you the way...
including routes and offline maps!

GET MORE OUT OF YOUR MARCO POLO GUIDE

IT'S AS SIMPLE AS THIS

1 go.marco-polo.com/jap

2 download and discover

GO!

WORKS OFFLINE!

SYMBOLS

INSIDER TIP Insider Tip

★ Highlight

●●●● Best of ...

☼ Scenic view

Ⓦ Responsible travel: fair
trade principles and the
environment respected

PRICE CATEGORIES HOTELS

Expensive over 24,000 yen

Moderate 18,000–
24,000 yen

Budget under 18,000 yen

The prices are for one double
room per night with breakfast

**PRICE CATEGORIES
RESTAURANTS**

Expensive over 6600 yen

Moderate 3000–6600 yen

Budget under 3000 yen

The prices are for one main
course or meal at midday,
they are often significantly
higher in the evening

CONTENTS

DID YOU KNOW?
Timeline → p. 14
Local specialities → p. 28
For bookworms and film buffs → p. 56
Empty orchestra → p. 62
Ryokan → p. 65
Public holidays → p. 133
Budgeting → p. 139
Weather → p. 140

MAPS IN THE GUIDEBOOK
(148 A1) Page numbers and coordinates refer to the road atlas
(0) Site/address located off the map Coordinates are also given for places that are not marked on the road atlas
(U A1) Coordinates for the map of Tokyo
Nara → p. 158
Kamakura → p. 158
Kyoto → p. 159

Nikko → p. 159
Osaka → p. 160

(🛏 A–B 2–3) refers to the removable pull-out map
(🛏 a–b 2–3) refers to the additional inset map on the pull-out map

INSIDE FRONT COVER:
The best highlights

INSIDE BACK COVER:
Map of Tokyo

3 1326 00537 1416

The best MARCO POLO Insider Tips

Our top 15 Insider Tips

INSIDER TIP **Always the latest thing**
Computer games, gadgets and Cosplay Cafés – the Tokyo quarter of *Akihabara* is the ultimate technology mecca. Be the first to explore the trends → p. 60

INSIDER TIP **Secrets of the geishas**
Have a glimpse at the world of the "Ladies of the Arts" (see right) on a nocturnal guided tour of the traditional Gion quarter in Kyoto → p. 74

INSIDER TIP **Only the best of everything**
At the beginning of the 20th century, a wealthy silk merchant from Yokohama built up a collection of architectural treasures in the fabulous gardens of *Sankei-in* that can be visited today → p. 65

INSIDER TIP **Fine beef for average earners**
Try this fine beef without it costing you an arm and a leg. The *Kobe Plaisir* in Kobe serves Kobe Beef at moderate prices → p. 73

INSIDER TIP **Time for tea**
Enjoy a cup of green tea and dream of old Kyoto on the cobbled streets of *Sannenzaka* and *Ninenzaka* → p. 79

INSIDER TIP **Close to the water**
Where Japan becomes Mediterranean: treat yourself to a night at the *Busena Terrace Resort* on Okinawa → p. 110

INSIDER TIP **Kimonos on all the streets**
Japan's best garment is enjoying a comeback – especially when 21-year-olds celebrate their coming-of-age in January and parade the streets in their festive garments → p. 132

INSIDER TIP **Private and traditional**
Japanese lifestyle and elegance combine in the *machiyas* of Kyoto. The rebuilt townhouses are highly stylish accommodations → p. 18

BEST OF ...

FOR FREE

● **Imperial flowers**
You can visit the 52-ac gardens of the *Imperial Palace* in Tokyo all year round free of charge. The loveliest sights are the cherry blossom and azaleas in the spring, the roses in summer and the camellias in winter → p. 56

● **Fabulous views**
There are wonderful panoramic views of the city from the *Town Hall* in Tokyo. Unlike other lookout towers, there is no charge for the ride up or access to the observation deck on the 45th floor → p. 58

● **The gods of the travellers**
Sumiyoshitaisha shrine is one of Osaka's most significant religious sites, and offers protection for families and travellers. On New Year's Day, three million people pray not only for a successful year in general, but above all for safe and happy returns from other countries. Admission to the site, which also has a number of faithfully reproduced buildings, is free → p. 97

● **Whisky and water**
Even the free guided tour of the *Suntory Yamazaki Distillery* is an experience – and not just for whisky lovers! The highlight is, of course, the free sampling of various blends, but the water that is served with them is also a delight→ p. 18

● **Well-guided**
The locals in Tokyo's traditional and lively Asakusa district will give you a free guided tour of their quarter, which includes the famous *Asakusa Kannon Temple* (photo) and the *Nakamise-dori* shopping street → p. 55

● **Magnificent temple tour**
The *Hongan-ji Temples* in central Tokyo East (Higashi) and West (Nishi), with their impressive architecture, fabulously colourful interior and famous status, are a veritable delight for the eyes – and there's no charge for visiting → p. 78

●●●● Dots in guidebook refer to "Best of..." tips

ONLY IN JAPAN
Unique experiences

● *Healthy luxury*
Japanese elegance, a fabulous garden and excellent dining make a visit to the restaurant *Tofuya-Ukai* in Tokyo Tower an undeniably successful, hard-to-beat gustatory experience → p. 60

● *Large theatre*
Dramas about popular heroes and love stories, traditional plays and dances in fabulous costumes are performed at Tokyo's famous *Kabuki-za* theatre. The all-male performers enjoy pop star status in Japan (photo) → p. 62

● *Sporting spectacle*
Despite the numerous scandals surrounding it, the Japanese love their national sport: sumo wrestling. The atmospheric highlights of this 2000-year-old wrestling match include the summer tournament at the *Aichi Prefectural Gymnasium* in Nagoya → p. 50

● *Pure Japan*
The wooden terrace of *Kiyomizu Temple*, which is supported by hundreds of pillars, is one of Japan's landmarks, and has the loveliest views of Kyoto → p. 79

● *Tea ceremony "lite"*
Chado, the "Way of tea", is a stylish pastime and Japanese work of art. Even if you have no prior knowledge and haven't spent hours sitting with your legs crossed, you can experience the special atmosphere during a half-hour tea ceremony at the *Happo-en* garden restaurant in Tokyo → p. 62

● *Empty orchestra*
Karaoke is a collective form of entertainment for the Japanese that foreigners are also welcome to share. One venue is the *JoyJoy* in Nagoya → p. 50

● *In silent remembrance*
The terrors and horrors of an atom bomb will forever be associated with the name Hiroshima. The *Peace Memorial Park* in the middle of the city is an extremely emotional memorial to the very first time an atomic bomb was dropped on humanity → p. 70

ONLY IN

BEST OF ...

● Jump right in
The *Aquarium Kaiyukan* in Osaka is the biggest aquarium in the world, with 27 pools. The central basin, which is 9 m/25.5 ft deep, is also home to two whale sharks and manta rays (photo) → p. 131

● On and under one roof
People watch, shop, dine and admire Osaka from a gondola 106 m/348 ft away! Experience life the Osaka way at the entertainment park *Hep Five* with over 100 boutiques and a Ferris wheel on the roof → p. 95

● Ride around Tokyo
Enjoy the views of Tokyo while riding the *Yamanote line*. The light greens trains of the JR circular railway travel clockwise and anti-clockwise around Tokyo in one-minute intervals. Almost each of the 29 stations has its own signature tune → p. 53

● Bathing Edo style
There are 16 different spas for you to splash around in at the *Oedo Onsen Monogatari* in Tokyo. A cotton kimono is worn in this vast complex, which is included in the admission. You can dine, shop, stroll around and easily bathe away a rainy day → p. 57

● Exotic taste experiences
Sample the foods and culinary creations that are typical of the famous Kyoto cuisine in the covered hall of *Nishiki Market* in Kyoto → p. 81

● Lost in comics
The Japanese manga are world famous. You can browse more than 40,000 issues of this uniquely Japanese comic at the *Kyoto International Manga Museum* → p. 80

RAIN

RELAX AND CHILL OUT
Take it easy and spoil yourself

● Hot spring with views
Not only can you relax in the hot spring of the *Sawada-koen-Rotem-buro Onsen* on Izu peninsula, but you can also enjoy the fabulous views from a cliff high above the Pacific Ocean → p. 65

● Pirate ship near Mount Fuji
In *Hakone*, colourful ships sail across picturesque Lake Ashi from Togendai to Hakone-machi and Moto-Hakone and back. They look like pirate ships or Mississippi paddle steamers. But despite – or perhaps because of – the kitsch and the lovely surroundings of Mount Fuji, the trip is an experience → p. 42

● Gentle attack on the senses
Treat yourself to a night in a traditional inn, a ryokan (photo). The scent of the tatami mats, the interior, the wonderful garden, the excellent service and the chefs in Kyoto's *Yoshikawa Inn* are hard to beat → p. 86

● Pampering by the ladies of the arts
Geishas are perfect hostesses and entertainers. A geisha evening can be both relaxing and expensive. Tip: Visit the *maikos* – trainee geishas – at the *Gion Kobu-Kaburenjo* in Kyoto. The differences are not usually obvious to the layman → p. 85

● Meditative floral art
Ikebana is much more than making artistic arrangements with flowers: the harmonious composition of lines is a form of meditation. Why not go on a course to learn the basic principles, perhaps at the *Sogegtsu Ikebana School* in Tokyo-Aoyama → p. 62

● Global bathing fun
Spa World in Osaka is the biggest spa complex in the world, with water landscapes from every continent, various treatment rooms, restaurants and – of course – quiet zones, and it's relatively inexpensive → p. 97

11

INTRODUCTION

DISCOVER JAPAN!

People who travel to Japan are usually looking for that special something in its exotic nature, its technology, its food and traditions. They want to experience how an entire nation can immerse itself in the collective intoxication of the *cherry blossoms*, and how the late-autumn leaves bathe its temples and gardens in a riot of colour. Visitors who are prepared to fly the long distance to the island kingdom want to relax in *hot springs*, enjoy the freshest raw fish, travel on the world's most punctual train, the Shinkansen bullet train, experience the symbiosis between architecture, nature and man in its *stylish gardens*, and gain an insight into the future in its noisy high-tech districts. As a guest, you will meet extremely *polite people* and be amazed at just how well everyone gets along in perfect harmony in such confined spaces.

Japan is wonderful. "I found here what I had hoped to find in Japan," wrote Nobel laureate Saul Bellow in the visitors' book of the exclusive *Tawara-ya* in Kyoto, "the human scale, tranquillity and beauty." And rare is the man who will not instantly find himself lost in dreams when beautifully dressed and made-up *geishas* promise them, "We still treat men like kings". The silky kimono also transforms "normal" women into porcelain figurines, little girls into colourful butterflies. And although

Japan's most photographed landmark: the red wooden gate of the shrine island of Miyajima

teenagers wear dull school uniforms every day, in their spare time they opt for the *wackiest outfits* in the world.

The Japanese have adapted. They have learnt to simply overlook any unpleasant realities. They understand how to find pleasure in a little flower – even if it is growing in a crack in the concrete on the high street outside their window. And they are nice. It is rare for foreign visitors to find a reason to complain about any rudeness on the part of the locals. They are always *courteous* to the numerous visitors to their country. Their guiding rule: you are most welcome, but please observe our rules. This applies in particular if the visitor heads straight for the heart of the world of Nippon's sons and daughters, such as the *communal baths* or a shoe-free restaurant.

Japan is different. Even modern Japanese are convinced that *gaijin* – foreigners – will never understand them completely. And there is no denying that there is much about the country that is strange. One-third of that is instantly obvious; the second is gradually discovered if you keep your eyes open, while the rest is almost impossible

Approx. 10 000–300 BC
Jomon culture The first settlements

300–710
First Tenno Dynasty

710–794
Nara era. Buddhism becomes the state religion

794–1185
Heian era. Foundation of Kyoto, birth of Japanese literature, formation of the Samurai caste

1477–1573
Senguko period, the "Warring States Period". 100 years of civil war in the country

1587
Persecution of Christians starts

14

to explain. The *cultural differences* demand a great deal of sensitivity. Would you like a better hotel room for the same price? Don't expect your tour leader or the receptionist to spontaneously make a decision in your favour for something that isn't already planned. The most you can expect is for them to take the matter further. In Japan, even the tiniest details are decided by *collective consensus*, and it is extremely unusual to know who is actually responsible for a decision.

The Far Eastern island location, and probably even more its *long years of political isolation*, have resulted in a relatively homogeneous mentality, a social structure that has developed almost without interruption, an almost tangible national history, and a highly refined culture. And yet Japan is multi-cultural. No one can say, with absolute certainty, where the nation originated – China, Korea, Siberia or Polynesia? Almost none of the art or culture for which Japan is (quite rightly) famous today – the *complicated script*, its delicate porcelain, the exclusive lacquer or the elegant kimono – would be possible without foreign influence.

Japan is rich – at least according to the statistics, with one of the highest per capita incomes in the world. Almost 90 percent of its population of approximately 126 million people consider themselves

> **Highly refined culture and multi-cultural**

as being "upper middle-class". And yet the country is not without, to some extent, its share of *hidden misery*. It is not unusual for the homeless to find refuge in cardboard boxes in the parks or along the rivers of major cities. And something else that is clear: Japan's consumer society can occasionally overlook its losers.

Japan has had its share of horrors – not only from the atomic bombs dropped on Hiroshima and Nagasaki, but also from *forces of nature* and human failure. On 11 March 2011, the north-east of the country experienced an earthquake of a magnitude of 9.0, something that had never been measured before. Minutes later, a murderous tsunami hit the coast, and only days later a nuclear disaster threatened. No one who experienced it will ever forget the worst disaster of the century, the *Pacific killer wave*, the frightening reactor ruins of the damaged NPP, the danger of a maximum credible nuclear accident so narrowly missed by this Far Eastern industrial power.

1603	1641	1868	1910	1937	1941
Tokugawa Ieyasu becomes Shogun, and is based in Edo (Tokyo). The Tenno is deposed. Beginning of the Edo period	Total isolation from other countries	Start of the Meji restoration. End of the Shogun Dynasty and isolation	Japan occupies Korea	Invasion of China	The Pacific War starts with the attack on Pearl Harbour

After that, it seemed as if nothing would ever be the same again. The direct damage and immediate production losses were put – conservatively – at somewhere around 265 billion £/342 billion US$. They affected a country whose politics initially seemed *paralysed*. But in the meantime, the Japanese nation has made an amazing recovery. And although this dramatic chapter is by no means history, it no longer features in the daily lives of the rest of the nation. Tourists can now travel easily all over the country – including into the prefecture of Fukushima.

> **It's loveliest at cherry blossom time and in the autumn, when the leaves change colour**

Japan is reinventing itself. Religious beliefs and standards have been completely re-thought since the shock of Fukushima. What makes life worth living? The *sixteen-hour day* of the busy worker bee, the factory as a substitute family? Is the government really always right? And not least: is nuclear power really safe, and does it make us strong? Nippon's trusting sons and daughters, who put their faith in technology, are deeply unsettled, starting to question their existence and the life philosophy behind it. And even in this otherwise harmony-loving country, *criticism and doubt* are suddenly on everyone's lips.

Japan can handle crises. For about two decades, what is now the world's third-biggest economy remained in depression, recession and deflation. The change only came in 2012, with the re-election of the liberal-democratic Prime Minister Shinzō Abe 2012 and his expansive monetary *economic policy*. Industry and politics are finally working together; unemployment is low, wages and salaries on the rise, and strikes are almost unheard of.

Japan is opening up. Tourism is booming in the oriental island empire, more than ever before. Every year, millions of Asians, and in particular Chinese, visit the traditional sights – in particular the *mega metropolises* of Tokyo and Osaka. However, this also means increases in the costs of flights, trains and hotel rooms. But by the same token, it is easier to travel around the country than you would perhaps expect of this 3000 km/1900 mi long archipelago. A tight network of airlines and bullet trains makes it easy to get to anything the island empire has to offer. The somewhat

1945
Atomic bombs dropped on Hiroshima and Nagasaki, Japan capitulates. Although Emperor Hirohito has to refuse the traditional claim to godliness of the Japanese Tenno, the US occupying forces do not insist on him going before an International Court of Justice

1947
Democratic constitution comes into effect, free voting and establishment of a government

1989
Tenno Akihito (Heisei era) accedes to the throne

1995
Earthquake in Kobe

Tokyo's trendy quarter The city's youth and mega screens meet at Shibuya station

subtropical climate can be challenging at times, and July and August in particular can be very hot. The best time to visit Japan is at cherry blossom time in March and April, and again when the leaves start to turn colour between October and December.

Although the *Japanese language* and script are a challenge, English is widely understood and spoken. Many of the signs in the major cities and conurbations have been translated. And if in doubt, you can always try communicating non-verbally using *gestures and pointing*. One thing you can be sure of: people will always be pleased to help you. And you can also be sure that this travel adventure will be well worthwhile: you will be absolutely fascinated by the island empire in the Far East!

> **Hot springs and high-tech quarters**

2002 Football World Cup in Japan and Korea

2006 Birth of Prince Hisato, first male child to be born into the Imperial House of Japan in four decades

2010 Nara celebrates the 1300th anniversary of becoming the capital "Heijo-kyo"

2011 Disaster of the century record-breaking earthquake, tsunami and damaged NPP in Fukushima

2020 Olympic Summer Games in Tokyo from 24 July to 9 August

WHAT'S HOT

1 Whisky world champion

High-proof Long the source of amusement for their unusual drinking habits – they like their whisky with plenty of water and on a mountain of ice cubes – the Japanese have now also made it to the top of this industry. Single malts from Yamazaki (*photo*) have what whisky expert Jim Murray describes as a "nutty, thick, dry taste ... as rounded as a snooker ball". The elegant drink is distilled in a somewhat unassuming village between Osaka and Kyoto at the ● *Suntory Yamazaki Distillery*. Guided tours are offered (*Mon–Fri 10am–3pm, Sat/Sun 10am–midday | Admission free | www.suntory.com/factory/yamazaki*) so you can see the distillery and sample the whisky. There is also a museum and a large shop.

2 Ramen and raw fish

Favourite restaurants INSIDER TIP Where Tokyo's renowned chefs themselves go to dine: Shinobu Namae of *L'Effervescence*, holder of two Michelin stars for his Japanese-French cuisine, likes to treat himself to the ramen soups served at *Usagi* near Shinsen railway station in his spare time. And to follow them with an espresso at the *Café Bleu* at famous Hachiko junction in Shibuya. Yuji Imaizumi of the raw fish establishment Sushi Sora at the *Mandarin Oriental* is holder of the *Obana* in Arakawa for the best eel restaurant in Tokyo, and recommends its *Usaku*, grilled eel with vinegar sauce. Unfortunately, it's very small and does not take bookings – so you'll have to queue for your eel.

3 Wooden houses

Stylish accommodation in Kyoto In bygone days, merchants, tradesmen and artists used to live and work in INSIDER TIP *Machiyas* (*photo*), the traditional townhouses of Kyoto. Today, most of these usually two-storey wooden buildings with the tiny gardens are being converted into luxurious lodgings *(www.kyoto-machiya-inn.com)*. The special architecture and exclusive interiors – an elegant combination of traditional and modern Japanese – creates the feeling of being "in the middle" of historic Kyoto. The machiyas are not cheap, but they accommodate between four and six people, and are also furnished and equipped for longer stays.

Street fashion

Hotspot Harajuku Young, cool, funky and from fabulous to eccentric: in Harajuku, one trend comes hot on the heels of another. The Tokyo quarter is an international hotspot for Street Fashion, and trend scouts from all over the world come to its streets and countless boutiques for ideas and inspiration. At the weekend, shopping fans are drawn in particular to the Takeshita-dori and its new landmark, a large *Daiso shop (daily from 10am–9pm)* where everything costs 100 yen.

Heavenly Tokyo

Sky Bars The sky bars and lounges in Tokyo's new skyscrapers try to outdo each other with their well-mixed drinks and breathtaking views. There are spectacular views from the rooftop bar at the *Andaz Hotel (daily from 5pm-midnight | Toranomon Hills | www.tokyo.andaz. hyatt.com/en/hotel/dining/rooftop-bar.html)* on the 52nd floor, while other top addresses within sight are the *TwentyEight (daily from 8am until midnight | Shiodome | www.conrad tokyo.co.jp/twentyeight)* (photo), the bar and lounge of the Conrad Hotel on the 28th floor, which serves afternoon tea and live music, and has unbeatable views of the Hamarikyu Gardens, the Rainbow Bridge and Tokyo Bay. The best addresses at a glance: *www.timeout.jp/en/tokyo/feature/10349/Tokyos-best-bars-with-a-view.*

IN A NUTSHELL

AMAE

Nothing describes the Japanese soul more aptly. The translation of amae is something like feeling as you did when you were a tiny child, being nursed by your mother. It is a form of fundamental trust, the feeling of being taken care of, being the object of another's kindness, unforced and uninhibited. Amae can only be achieved in the closest group dynamic, a kind of inner circle that is like a mystical association.

This deeply-felt comfort is experienced with one's family or neighbours, and later on at school or in a club. Without amae, a Japanese man might be able to live with his wife and child but would never survive at work. He needs a specific place in society. That is the key to many of his peculiarities, such as the open rejection of individualism which in this country is often interpreted as egotism and being an outsider. Even young school children learn that "You hit on a nail that sticks out".

BONSAI

"Everything in Japan is small – you only have to look at bonsai." Be honest: don't you agree? And in fact, you wouldn't be entirely wrong. It's true that the lack of space in the cities forces people to forget about having a garden of their own. But growing bonsai is, above all, an art that feeds entire villages. A miniature Japanese pine or tangerine tree as a souvenir of your travels? A lovely idea, and the carefully trimmed trees can even

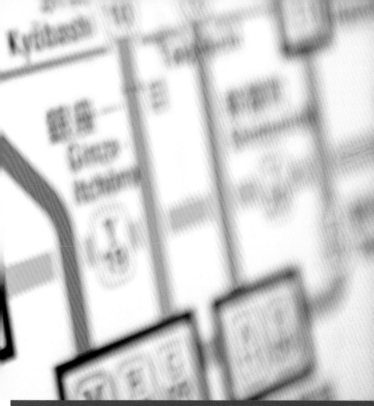

Puffer fish and amae, geishas, mangas and genko – Japan has plenty of surprises for visitors

go in your hand luggage. But be careful! The trees might be tiny, but the price for old bonsai in particular are quite the opposite.

FORCES OF NATURE

The Japanese are certainly aware that they live on an atoll of earthquakes, tsunami, hurricanes and volcanoes – even if they choose to ascribe them to fate. Every month, an average of 73 quakes measuring level 4 or higher shake the island empire, and there are approxi-

mately 1.7 measuring a dangerous 6 or higher every year. The worst earthquake measured so far was the force 9 Fukushima seaquake off the north-east coast on 11 March 2011. The massive quakes were followed by a devastating tsunami that reduced entire settlements to rubble, grabbing houses, cars and ships with it or burying them under the wreckage. This natural disaster caused around 21,000 deaths and missing. Fishermen thought up the word "tsunami" many centuries ago, when they returned to the coast after their fishing trips and found their harbours had been devastated by a spring tide even though everything seemed calm and quiet on the open sea. The natural

last erupted on 16 September 1707, the 3776-m/12,388-ft crater has recently been judged potentially seismically active again.

A manga for all seasons: readers of all ages enjoy the japanese version of the comic

phenomenon is caused by strong vibrations on the ocean floor, and can result in waves up to 40 m/131.2 ft high.

Hurricanes are tropical tornadoes in the north-western part of the Pacific combined with torrential downpours and flooding. In the 13th century, a hurricane even prevented Japan from being conquered by the fleets of the Chinese Mongolian emperors, as the violent storm forced them to turn back. There is also the permanent risk of volcanic eruptions in Japan. Of the 265 volcanoes along the island chain, around 40 are classed as active. The highest of them is Japan's holy mountain, Fuji, around 100 km/62 mi from Tokyo. Although it

FUGU

An invitation to a fugu meal has an apparently dangerous after-taste. Having said that, consumption of puffer fish – at least in a speciality restaurant – isn't necessarily a form of "Japanese roulette". It has been a very long time since anyone died of fugu poisoning.

Only fish chefs with a special license are permitted to work with this expensive delicacy. They have spent years learning how to wield their knives without damaging the liver or other internal parts of the puffer fish, which could contain deadly tetrodotoxin. But in fact, it is usually the toso fugu that is served, which is hardly ever contaminated.

GEISHA

Most tourists speak highly of the geishas they photograph on the streets of Kyoto, although in fact they are usually *maikos*, trainee geishas. Dressed in their costumes and carefully made-up, the maikos come extremely close to the Japanese ideal of perfect beauty – an oval face with cherry-red lips, eyebrows like half-moons, flawless white complexion, hair as black as pitch, a long, sensuous neck and the gently rounded figure clad in a silk kimono.

Whereas geishas are booked for events, perhaps tea ceremonies in tea houses, the 16- to 20-year-old trainee geishas are not expected to be particularly skilled at dancing, singing or even conversation. They are booked just to be looked at, and are a popular photographic motif.

GENGO

Do not be surprised if you happen to see a year on an official document or restaurant bill that you are unable to identify. It was most probably dated according to *Gengo*, the so-called imperial calendar. People who were born in 1950 will have *Showa 25* on their birth certificate, after the era of Emperor Hirohito. When he died on 7 January 1989, the 64th year of *Showa* (bright peace) ended after only six days. This was followed by the tenure of Emperor Akihito, and with it the era of *Heisei* (peace everywhere). Japan began the new millennium in the 13th year of *Heisei*. But most people will also understand you if you say 2001.

HIKIKOMORI

This is the name in Japan for the social phenomenon of young people who become withdrawn, shut themselves away. At some point they stop leaving their rooms and break off all social contacts, sometimes for years or decades. They earn no money and live with their parents – who often can only watch helplessly, or else are too ashamed to talk about their "failure children". Many hikikomori spend their time playing video games, surfing the Internet, "devouring" mangas and watching endless TV. If they do ever venture outside, it's usually at night.

MANGA

They already account for 40 percent of all printed products in Japan: mangas. The Japanese version of the comic is popular with every social level; there are mangas for all ages, on every subject and for any sexual orientation. And there are subgroups. For young people, there are mangas for girls *(shojo)* and boys *(shonen),* and among adults for women *(josei)* and men *(seinen)* – the latter may be pornographic. Mangas and anime (cartoons) have been recognised as an independent art form in Japan since 2000. In Kyoto, there is even a faculty for mangas with adjoining museum.

MYSTICISM

Friday 13th leaves the Japanese cold. They have other superstitions. In Japan, the lunar calendar, *Rokki*, governs important decisions. The day that is most feared is *Butsumetsu*. According to the Chinese-Japanese lunar calendar, this day – which means "the death of Buddha" – is considered the unluckiest of all days. In a six-day cycle, it lowers the mood and noticeably slows down activities. According to folk wisdom, important decisions should not be made on Butsumetsu, nor should there be any celebrations. And as you would expect, Butsumetsu is not usually chosen for wedding ceremonies. Most couples will wait until *Taian* – the lucky day that promises the most favourable conditions five or six times a month.

SAMURAI

Although there have not been any Samurai for some 150 years now, many Japanese still like to behave like them today – at least in their imagination. The members of the warrior caste, who eschew business, money and emotions, were considered loyal agents of the feudal lords, organising factors and elite warriors at the same time – the name is derived from the word *samurau* (to serve). Their superior commander is the *Shogun* – in the Middle Ages often the Emperor's political opponent.

The self-image of a Samurai included a code of honour that was developed and refined over the course of centuries into the law-like *Bushido*, the way of the warrior, peaking with the highest form of ritual suicide *seppuku* (usually called *hara-kiri* in the west).

SHINTOISM

The Japanese have an excellent arrangement with their Shinto gods. No house can be inaugurated, no contract signed without their blessing. No taxi may transport its first passenger without first being purified by the deities. Whereas Christianity is of secondary importance in Japan and Islam does not feature at all, Buddhism, as the "second religion" and of equal standing, is responsible for anything and everything concerning death. Life, however, is Shintoism.

Especially when money is involved, there is plenty of praying and lots of donating. Someone wanting a business matter to go well will pray to Inari, who – originally the god of rice, the country's most important food – is today responsible for wealth. Every day thousands of people make the pilgrimage to the *Zeni-arai Benten*, the money-"laundering" temple of Kamakura, to wash money in the spring waters, which is said to do anything from double it to increase it a hundredfold.

TENNO

Japan's emperor is neither a ruling monarch nor a head of state, nor a living god – well, not any more since Emperor Hirohito eschewed this claim in 1945. The constitution describes the Keeper of the Chrysanthemum Throne as a "symbol of the State and the unity of the people". Because no one is entirely sure what this means, discretion is used in the interpretation of the imperial role. However, it is agreed that almost 2700 years of continuous imperial rule since the first emperor, Jimmu (supposedly 660 BC) and his 124 successors (to date) are strong evidence of the continuity of the Japanese nation.

The current Emperor Akihito, who was enthroned in 1989 and was the first Tenno to marry a commoner, is not often seen in public. Twice a year, once on his birthday on 23 December and at New Year, he appears to be celebrated by the people, and occasionally he performs official functions and travels on state visits. The court works hard to ensure that the Tenno, as a "person above the clouds" is never a topic of discussion.

THE "HERBIVORE" GENERATION

Almost 50 percent of all single female Japanese aged between 18 and 34 prefer to be on their own. Their male counterparts are even more commitment-resistant. More than 61 percent of single male Japanese don't even have a girlfriend.

In particular, the lack of interest on the part of Japanese men is causing demographers some concern because of the ageing society. The issue has even been given a name: the "Herbivore Generation" *(soshokukei danshi)* – although it has nothing at all to do with vegetarians. It is a play on words, because sexual relations are known as carnal relations.

Likelihood of flirting? Not really. In the mood for romance? Nope! Feel like partying? Hardly. Interested in sex? Ditto.

ual freedom. Work and hobbies were more important to them than a secure relationship or even marriage.

THE MAN IN THE MACHINE

Not exactly what you would expect! Stand helplessly at the ticket machine in the vast Tokyo Metro, then look at the

Even children who are just starting school are taught what to do in the event of an earthquake

Japan's youth is increasingly shutting itself off from the opposite sex. Recent studies have confirmed that Nippon's daughters and sons prefer a solitary life out of principle. Half of the respondents stated that they were not at all interested in a love relationship, not even a date. They were not interested in having a deep, intimate relationship with the opposite sex; it would only take up time and restrict their individ-

long queue behind you before pressing the "Help" button, and you will simply not believe your eyes. After being asked to "Wait a moment, please", a hatch opens between two modern ticket machines and out pops a real human face! Next, a friendly person may even come out of a narrow door and help a confused passenger to find the right colour for the right train on the vast display board. What service!

25

FOOD & DRINK

If you would like to see just what it is that makes Japan's dining culture what it is, start with a typical breakfast. Miso soup with fresh algae and tofu, rice, pickled vegetables, grilled cold fish and green tea are the standards.

Foreigners might find this selection takes a little getting used to, but it does reflect the foundations of Japanese cuisine that, for a long time, had to contend with what the barren territory of this isolated island kingdom had to offer: *seafood, vegetables and rice*. This spartan and extremely idiosyncratic diet is still the choice of older and health-conscious Japanese today, and is also the reason why life expectancy in Japan is the highest anywhere in the world. But since the economic miracle,

Nippon's gastronomy has exploded and opened up to the West. You will find any culinary choice and regional cuisine. In Tokyo alone, you have the choice of 160,000 restaurants and, thanks to the Japanese commitment to *perfection and lightness*, many dishes actually taste better than in their countries of origin. Tokyo often receives more stars in the Michelin Guide than anywhere else – around twice as many as in Paris. From the culinary aspect, Japan's own specialities are undeniably *exciting and adventurous*. The choice is surprisingly extensive – ranging from rustic, inexpensive *noodle soups* to the aristocratic *kaiseki*. With the exception of exclusive restaurants, most of the pubs and bars observe the rather nice habit of display-

Photo: Something of everything – kaiseki cuisine

Nippon's gastronomy is independent and unique, but has opened up to the West – and above all, only the very best is ever served up

ing a *plastic image* of their dishes and the prices in their windows. It has to be said, though, that the portions in the pictures are usually bigger.

The main ingredient in Japanese cuisine is fish. The classics are *sushi or sashimi*, both made with raw fish and loved all over the world. Of course, the freshest catches are to be found on the *Tokyo Fish Market*, the biggest in the world. More than 400 restaurants, food stands and shops open there at 5.30am. Fish and vegetables are also the ingredients

of *tempura*. This speciality, which the Portuguese brought to Japan, is deep-fried. Tempura is made with shrimps, fish fillets and various raw vegetables such as lotus, peppers, sweet potatoes and shiitake mushrooms that are dipped in a light batter and then quickly deep fried.

The guest dips the pieces served in a basket in a light soy sauce that is seasoned with radish and ginger.

Japanese haute cuisine is undoubtedly *kaiseki*. This multi-course dinner consists

LOCAL SPECIALITIES

DISHES

Kaiseki – tiny seasonal treats that also delight the eye

Ramen – Chinese noodle soup with meat, vegetables, miso or soy sauce (photo left)

Soba – buckwheat noodles, either served as a hot soup in vegetable stock or cold in soy sauce

Sukiyaki – wafer-thin slices of beef and vegetables cooked in an iron pot in soy sauce and red wine, then whisked with an egg

Sushi, sashimi – raw fish (photo right) on cold pickled rice balls (sushi) or alone (sashimi)

Teppanyaki – fillet steak cooked on a hot plate in front of the guests and cut into bite-sized pieces; dipped in soy sauce with horseradish

Tonkatsu – breaded pork escalope in a special sauce, chopped cabbage and mustard

Udon – rather thick, soft wheat flour noodles

Yakitori – pieces of chicken on bamboo skewers with onions or pepper grilled over an open fire and brushed with sauce

DRINKS

Beer – Japan's favourite drink; the well-known brands Asahi, Kirin, Suntory and Sapporo are also popular with European connoisseurs

Green tea – drunk hot or cold, more recently also with milk and sugar or lemon

Sake – rice wine, served hot or cold depending on the season, and usually straight up

Shochu – 20-to 45-percent alcohol by volume distilled from rice and sweet potatoes. It is also drunk with water or soda and lemon

of a large number of small dishes, and embodies the three *ideals of Japanese cuisine* – good taste, decorative presentation and elegant dishes – and is therefore considered the ultimate in the country's cooking art. No doubt because of its isolated island location, and possibly also for religious reasons, meat was not seen for a long time. However, in recent decades, the Japanese have developed their very own delicacies such as *teppanyaki*, *shabu shabu* and *sukiyaki*. One particular example is marbled Japanese beef, usually known as *kobe*. Unfortunately, it is very expensive. Visitors also greatly appreciate *shabu shabu* and *sukiyaki*. In both cases, the waiter serves plates of raw, wafer-thin slices of beef with vegetables, mushrooms and tofu. The diner uses chopsticks to dip the former in a copper kettle of hot broth, then in peanut and sesame or soy sauce. With *sukiyaki*, meat and vegetables are quickly fried in an iron pot, then cooked with soy sauce and rice wine and a raw egg stirred in.

Noodles are a special but internationally less well-known chapter in Japanese cuisine. Many Japanese are positively addicted to *soba*, *udon* or *ramen*, and will happily eat them (usually cooked in stock) at any time of day. Many *noodle establishments* are even open at night. You'll find them on almost any street, and prices are low.

The range of prices can be quite adventurous, and may often cause a tummy-ache in foreign guests. For an *inexpensive meal* eat at lunchtime. In cities like Tokyo and Osaka in particular (less so in the tourist centres such as Kyoto), the tremendous competition and long economic crisis have resulted in well-priced set lunches. Office workers with lower incomes eat (usually very well) in the INSIDERTIP smaller pubs and restaurants in city office towers, often found in the basements. In the evenings, prices in the same establishments may well triple. This is the tradition, because the evening meal is generally at the company's expense.

Japan is also international when it comes to drinks, offering the entire range from French mineral water to German *beer*. The offer of alcoholic drinks has also been internationalised in recent years — the choice of wines and spirits (in cities) leaves little to be desired, and prices have become more moderate. Beer has long been a favourite, along with *sake*, and is available everywhere, even in the tiniest village pub.

Inexpensive: lunch at the bar with a beer

SHOPPING

The shopping in Japan is world class: the offers, service, quality and opening hours are all just right – all the major shops are open until 8pm at the weekends. If only it weren't for the many zeroes on the price labels – this consumer paradise is horribly expensive.

ART

Some of the most popular souvenirs are old woodcuts (*ukiyoe*). They have even provided inspiration for European painters such as Vincent van Gogh. *Ukiyo-e* means "pictures of the flowing world", and refers only to scenes from the Edo period with courtesans, theatres or geisha houses. The romantic landscape paintings by Ando Hiroshige (1779–1858) and Katsushika Hokusai (1760–1849) are famed beyond the country's borders. However, original prints, which are available from art shops, are very expensive. But inexpensive, high quality prints of all famous works are available.

ARTS AND CRAFTS

Japanese paper (*washi*) is considered the finest hand-made paper in the world. The offer in specialist shops and department stores ranges from gift wrap and writing paper in bright colours to boxes in glowing colours and skilfully-made folded paper art (*origami*). The lacquered goods (*shikki*) are fabulous. Japan's artists have turned this technique, which they learnt from the Chinese, into undeniable mastery. The objects include utility items such as soup or rice dishes, trays and chopsticks, but also furniture and ornaments. Exquisite lacquerware consisting of up to 60 layers from the top addresses of Kyoto or Wajima, which use much silver and gold dust, is very expensive. However, more affordable items such as chopsticks, trays and sake beakers are also available. Japanese ceramics, which delight for their simple aesthetics, also have an excellent reputation. Since the development of the tea ceremony from about 1333, the cups in particular have become highly coveted collectors' items.

Japanese dolls make pretty souvenirs, although they are only meant to be looked at. The ladies have highly ornate hairstyles and are dressed in elegant kimonos, while the men are dressed as Samurai. The offer for INSIDER TIP ▶ Dolls'

State-of-the-art electronics, used kimonos and exclusive crafts – Japan is a shopping paradise

or Girls' Day on 3 March is especially large, when the department stores display the imperial couple's royal household on the black lacquered stairways.

CLOTHING

Apart from T-shirts with motifs such as sushi dishes or amusing kanji symbols, the light cotton *yukatas* (summer kimonos) are best-sellers. Other popular purchases are the dark silk *haori* jackets that Nippon's elite males wear over their kimonos on special occasions. Kimono belts (*obi*) are also recommended – you can use them not least as highly decorative table runners. Bargains are also to be had in INSIDERTIP used wedding kimonos.

ELECTRONIC GOODS, CAMERAS

The Tokyo suburb of Akihabara is a mecca for "techies". There are more than 600 department and specialist stores offering every possible kind of electronic appliance, including ones not yet seen in Europe: from computers and digital cameras to video games. Special chains such as *Laox* offer tax-free goods tailored to foreign standards. Be sure to buy export items of 220V and to PAL standard. Japanese mobile phones do not work in Europe. In Shinjuku, the *Yodobashi* department store has the biggest range of photo technology and office electronics with over 30,000 items. *BIC Camera* near the Ginza is another no. 1 address.

LUCKY CHARMS

The Japanese are highly superstitious, and they love lucky charms. The offer in the temples is most impressive. Visitors can purchase chains of lucky charms there for almost any occasion: for the next test or exam, for good health, to be lucky in love, safe driving and much more.

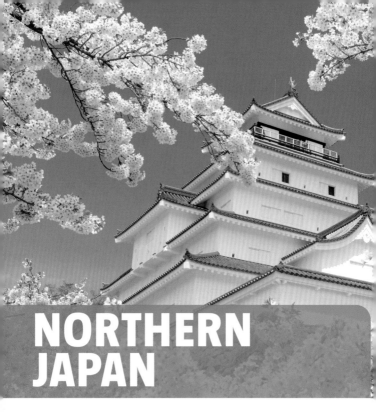

NORTHERN JAPAN

Travel to the north of Japan, and you'll think you're in a different world. The relatively quiet streets, plenty of nature, and the low population in particular distinguish the northern part of the main island Honshu, known as Tohoku, and the northernmost main island Hokkaido from most other parts of the country.

The conservation areas and skiing regions are vast, varied and relaxing. Hokkaido accounts for more than one-fifth of the total area of Japan, but its population is only five percent of the total.

The area was greatly affected by the natural disaster of 11 March 2011. Over 19,000 people were killed, and some 150,000 inhabitants of the Pacific coast had to be sheltered in emergency accommodation, even if only temporarily. After the quake, the tsunami and the damage to the NPP Fukushima came the economic disaster. Many people faced ruin. Today, you can safely travel anywhere in the country.

AIZU-WAKAMATSU

(151 D2–3) (꘭ G6) **The town (pop. 125,000) was once the centre of power of the influential Matsudaira clan that fought the imperial troops alongside the Shogun in 1867.**

After the defeat, Aizu-Wakamatsu burnt down in 1868. The collective suicide of

Lots of space and time, and not a lot of people – in northern Japan you'll find plenty of nature and some of Japan's loveliest scenery

the sons of the Samurai is legendary, and still affects the local patriotic sensitivities of the people of Aizu-Wakamatsu to this day.

SIGHTSEEING

INSIDER TIP ▶ SAMURAI RESIDENCE BUKE-YASHIKI

The impressive reconstruction of a Samurai residence with 35 rooms. *April–Nov 8.30am–5pm, Dec–March 9am–4.30pm | Admission 850 ¥ | Bus from Higashiyama Onsen railway station to Aizu Bukeyashiki-mae (approx. 35 min)*

TSURUGA CASTLE

Once Japan's strongest fortress and the heart of the town for over 600 years, it was destroyed in 1868. The complex was completely rebuilt in 2011. There is also a 400-year-old tea house in the castle grounds *(daily from 8.30am–5pm | Admission 200, combined ticket with castle 500 ¥)*, which escaped destruction. *Daily 8.30am–4.30pm |*

Nebuta Matsuri Festival in Aomori: a frenzy of lights, masks and sound

Admission 410 ¥ | Bus from railway stati-on to Tsuruga-jo kitaguchi

FOOD & DRINK/ WHERE TO STAY

SHIBUKAWA DONYA

Old Japanese restaurant. Local dried fish and herring specialities. Small ryokan next door. *Daily 11am–9pm | tel. 0242 28 40 00 | Budget*

INFORMATION

At the station (tel. 0242 32 06 88) and Aizu-Wakamatsu City Sightseeing (tel. 0242 39 12 51 | www.city.aizuwakamatsu. fukushima.jp)

AOMORI

(148 C5) *(Ⅲ H4)* **The capital (pop. 300,000) of the eponymous prefecture became famous for the archaeological** finds dating back to the Jomon period and the Seikan Tunnel, the world's longest undersea tunnel. Since 1988, it has connected Imabetsu (60 km/37.3 mi to the north) to Shiriuchi on Hokkaido.

The town is famous all over Japan for the INSIDER TIP *Nebuta Matsuri* Festival (early August), which attracts thousands of visitors who then dance through the town in a procession of wagons lit by giant lanterns. According to the legend, imperial troops in the 9th century wanted to lure in the clans to the north and conquer them. The *Nebuta-no-Sato Museum (daily 10am–5pm | Admission 630 ¥ | Bus from JR Aomori 30 min)* provides a very good impression of it – complete with festival carriage and daily performances. The attraction of the Tsugaru peninsula to the west of Aomori is the *Shirakami mountain region (Shirakami-Sanchi Visitor Center | daily Nov–June 9am–4.30pm, July–Oct 8am–5pm)* which, with its original beech forest, was declared a World Heritage Site and is particularly delightful in autumn, when the leaves change colour.

FOOD & DRINK

SAKANAKKUI NO DEN
Sushi, kaiseki and other Japanese dishes. *Mon–Sat 11.30am–2pm, 5pm–10pm | tel. 0177 32 25 80 | Budget*

WHERE TO STAY

JAL CITY AOMORI
Modern 3-star hotel, six minutes from the railway station. One storey is only for women. Free WLAN. *167 rooms | tel. 0177 32 25 80 | www.aomori-jalcity.co.jp | Budget*

INFORMATION

Tourist information: *ASPAM Building | tel. 0177 34 25 00 | en-aomori.com*

WHERE TO GO

MORIOKA (148 C6) *(ಐ H5)*
The capital of the Iwate prefecture (pop. 305,000) in the shadow of the 2041 m Namba Fuji mountain is a winter sports centre (180 km/112 mi from Aomori). This natural curiosity was declared a national treasure in 1923. The *Hoon-ji*, a Buddhist temple, is home to 500 lacquered statues of Buddha, images of Marco Polo and the Mongolian conqueror Kublai Khan. You can stay at the *Kumagai Ryokan (tel. 019 6 51 30 20 | kumagairyokan. com | Budget)*, a traditional guest house with a warm welcome for foreigners. *Morioka Tourist Information Centre | tel. 019 6 04 33 05 | www.city.morioka.iwate.jp*

TOWADA HACHIMANTAI NATIONAL PARK ★ (148 C5) *(ಐ H5)*
One of Japan's last wildernesses with volcanoes, steaming geysers, bubbling mud ponds, the Towada crater lake and the Hachimantai volcanic plateau. Mount Iwate (2038 m) is honoured as the "Fuji of the North", even though its two peaks are nothing like the original. The *Tamagawa Onsen* on the Hachimantai Plateau with its extremely hot, acidic, slightly radioactive water is considered one of the best medicinal springs in Japan. *Hachimantai Chojo* is the main starting point for excursions. Buses run from Morioka station *(by rail from Aomori)* to Hachimantai Chojo *(2 hour ride, not in winter | Ticket 1320 ¥ | www.hachimantai.jp)*. Excursion boats will take you from the tourist centres Yasumiya and Nenokuchi *(1300 ¥)* in 50 minutes. *Tourist Information at JR bus station | tel. 0177 231621*

NIIGATA

(150 C2) *(ಐ G6)* **The administrative seat of the eponymous prefecture (pop. 810,000) on the coast of the Japanese Sea is an important traffic hub.**
It's easy to get from here to the Japanese Alps and onto ferries, including to Sato. The railway station is also the terminus for the Joetsu Shinkansen of Tokyo Ueno. However, the city is also famous for the quality of its seafood and sake.

★ **Towada Hachimantai National Park**
Close to Aomori is one of Japan's best medicinal springs → p. 35

★ **Matsushima Bay**
Much celebrated by poets: the picturesque bay near Sendai → p. 39

MARCO POLO HIGHLIGHTS

SIGHTSEEING

HONCHO MARKET

Lively trading place for fruit, vegetables and seafood that covers several pedestrian arcades. Lots of little restaurants – a delight for the eyes and palate. *Mon–Sat 10am–5pm | At the centre of the Furumachi Arcade*

SHINANO GAWA

The banks of the longest river in Japan are the ideal spot from which to watch the locals go about their lives.

FOOD & DRINK

INAKAYA

Speciality restaurant for seafood and steamed fish on rice, popular with the locals, moderate prices. *Daily | Kyoban | tel. 025 2 23 12 66 | Budget*

WHERE TO STAY

HOTEL OKURA

Best hotel in town, next to Bandai Bridge with views of the river. *265 rooms | Chuo | tel. 025 2 24 61 11 | www.okura-niigata.com | Moderate*

INFORMATION

Tourist information: *Chuo | tel. 025 2 23 81 81 | www.nvcb.or.jp/en*

WHERE TO GO

SADO (150 C2) *(⊞ F–G6)*

In the feudal period, Japan's sixth-largest island (approx. 80 km/49.7 mi from Niigata) was an infamous penal colony for intellectual "undesirables". Today, the island's biggest charm is the leisurely lifestyle of its inhabitants in the remote fishing villages. But then there's also the annual (usually the third week in August) "Festival of the Earth" with three days of drumming and dancing. The famous Kodo Drummers of the village of Ogi spend eight months of the year on tour *(evening menu approx. 4000 ¥, lower-priced all-inclusive offers available through the organiser | tel. 0259 86 36 30 | www.kodo.or.jp)*. Book in plenty of time. Stay at the Ryokan Hotel *Yoshidaya (70 rooms | Ebisu | Sado Island, Niigata | tel. 0259 27 21 51 | www.japaneseguesthouse.com | Budget)* with sea views and onsen. *Information: Tourist Information Center | Niigata Station Bandai Exit | tel. 025 2 41 79 14*

There are ferries from Niigata to Ryotsu on Sado *(Jetfoil | travel time 1 hour | 6520 ¥ | other ferries: travel time 135 min | 2510 ¥ per route). www.visitsado.com/en*

SAPPORO

(148 C3) *(⊞ H3)* **The cosmopolitan capital (pop 1.9 million) Hokkaido, made world-famous for hosting the Winter Olympics in 1972 and the Football World Cup in 2002, delights with its friendly inhabitants and generous architecture.**

No other town in Japan is so clearly laid-out and surrounded by so much countryside. The blocks are arranged in all four directions starting from the TV tower.

SIGHTSEEING

ODORI PARK

It's impossible to miss the largest street, Odori Park, 105 m wide and stretching through the town from east to west. The annual Snow Festival takes place here every year at the beginning of February;

its sights include snow copies of famous buildings.

TOKEI-DA CLOCKTOWER

The bell tower *was* the first wooden construction built in the western style. Inside is a small local history museum *(Tue–Sun 9am–5pm | Admission 200 ¥ | Chuo).*

FOOD & DRINK

21 CLUB

Smart restaurant with wonderful views from the 25th floor. Speciality: teppanyaki. *Daily evenings, Sun/Sat lunchtimes | Novotel Hotel, 25 F | Chuo | tel. 011 5 61 10 00 | www.novotelsapporo.com | Moderate*

SAPPORO BEER GARDEN

Giant beer hall belonging to the native large brewery. The all-you-can-eat grill buffets are popular. *Daily | Chuo | tel. 011 7 42 15 31 | www.sapporo-bier-garten.jp | Budget*

WHERE TO STAY

HOTEL NEW OTANI SAPPORO

340-room luxury hotel with modern interior. *Chuo | tel. 011 2 22 11 11 | www. newotanisapporo.com | Moderate*

HOTEL NOVOTEL

Designer hotel in a good location and with the best service. *230 rooms | Chuo | tel. 011 5 61 10 00 | www.novotelsapporo. com | Moderate*

INFORMATION

You can find a town guide for Sapporo through the *Sapporo Tourist Information Centre (JR station | tel. 011 2 13 50 88).*

SAPPORO CITIZEN CONTACT CENTER

The information centre *(tel. 011 2 22 48 94 | www.welcome.city.sapporo.jp/ english)* is in a central location opposite the bell tower.

Snow Festival in Sapporo: The white fun is at your feet from the TV tower

WHERE TO GO

SHIKOTSU TOYA NATIONAL PARK
(148 C3) (*Ø H3*)
This 380-mi² national park is only 30 km/18.6 mi from Sapporo. The volcanic lake Toya is one of Japan's loveliest areas. The thermal spa resort on the southern edge of the lake is the region's tourism centre with several hotels offering public spas *(admission 500–1000 ¥)*. Tourist boats operate on the lake between May and October.

However, the area isn't without its risks: the volcano Usu is active, and last erupted in 2000. Several thousand people had to leave the region. A well-designed volcano museum with a 3D multi-vision cinema at *Toyako Visitor Center (Toyako Town)* provides information on the bubbling mountain *(daily 9am–5pm | Admission free | tel. 0142 75 25 55 | www.toyako-vc.jp)*. You can also admire Japan's youngest volcano, Showa Shin-zan, which was only formed in 1943.

Several buses travel from Toya station *(Toyaka | Abuta District | tel. 0142 75 24 46)* to the *Noribetsu Onsen*, 90 minutes away, and the Japanese people's most favourite thermal spa in Hokkaido *(www.takimotokan.co.jp)*. There are many baths and hotels with thermal baths, such as the *Daiichi Takimotokan Hotel (thermal baths daily 9am–6pm | admission 2000 ¥ | tel. 0143 84 21 11)*.

WINDSOR TOYA RESORT & SPA ⤲
The conference hotel of the G8 World Summit 2008 is situated on a mountain between Lake Toya and the Pacific. The views are breathtaking. Inside is a clever combination of cosmopolitan style and traditional Japanese elegance. *398 rooms | Shimizu Toyakocho Abutagun | tel. 0142 73 11 11 | www.windsorhotels.co.jp | Expensive*

LOW BUDGET

Hokkaido has more than 254 inexpensive camp-sites *(en.visit-hokkaido.jp/activities/camping sites)*. You can also rent a bungalow at the *Satsunai River Camp (Minami Satsunai | tel. 0155 69 43 78)*.

The hotel a *Otaru Villa Moun Teng (Otaru | tel. 0134 33 69 44)* at the foot of Mount Otaru is close to the town centre, and an excellent starting point for hiking or skiing.

A bus tour is only 100 ¥ *(Donan-Bus | tours: 21 Jan.–21 Feb, 20 June–15 Aug., 15–20 Oct | tel. 0142 75 23 51)* around Lake Toya with 18 stops.

SENDAI

(151 E2) (*Ø H6*) **Much of Tohoku's biggest town (pop. 100,000) was destroyed in WWII.**

The "Town of the forests", the hilltop mausoleum of town founder Masamune Zuihoden, is well worth a visit *(daily April–Oct 9am–4.30, Nov–March 9am–4pm | admission 550 ¥ | Loople bus from the railway station to stop no. 4)*.

FOOD & DRINK

INSIDER TIP SENDAI KAKITOKU
Famed for the "Kakitoku set" with fried oysters on rice and three different daily dishes. *Tue–Sun 11am–5pm | Ichiban | tel. 022 2 22 07 85 | Moderate*

WHERE TO STAY

MONTEREY SENDAI
This hotel is in a central location, only 100 m from the railway station, and

canic in origin. Often all you can see are the mountaintops with oddly-shaped trees above the water. The region was affected by the quake on 11 March 2011, as is movingly recorded in the Tourist In-

Bridge in Matsushima Bay: it leads to one of the 260 islands of volcanic origins

offers three restaurants and a spa with hot springs. *206 rooms | tel. 022 2 65 71 10 | www.hotelmonterey.co.jp/en/ htl/sendai | Budget*

INFORMATION

SENDAI TOURIST INFORMATION CENTER
JR Sendai Station | Chuo | tel. 022 2 22 40 69 | www.sentabi.jp/en/info

WHERE TO GO

MATSUSHIMA BAY ⭐ **(151 E2)** *(ɯ H6)*
The impressive bay with more than 260 pine-covered islands stretches from the tiny town 20 km/12.4 mi north-east of Sendai. It is one of the "Three Views of Japan". Most of the islands are vol-

formation Centre. The popularity of the exceptional scenery, much lauded by the country's most famous poets, is unbroken – and consequently overrun. Take the train to Shiogama or Matsushima Kaigan, from where you can get to the moorings for the tour boats.

It's just a five-minute walk from Matsushima Kaigan station along a Japanese maple-lined alley to the *Zuiganji (April–Sept daily 8am–5pm, Oct–March 8am–3.30pm | admission 700 ¥)*, one of the loveliest Zen temples in the north. The painted screens and woodcuttings in the mail hall are well worth a visit. The site, which was founded in 827, is being refurbished until 2018, so is only partly opened. *Information: tel. 022 3 54 26 18 | www.matsushima-kanko.com/en*

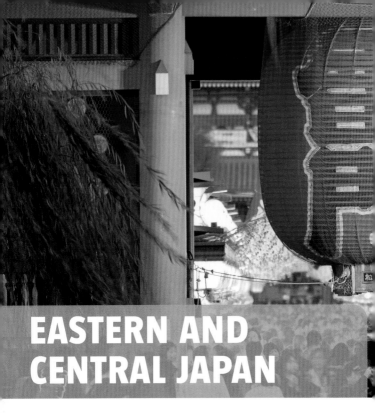

EASTERN AND CENTRAL JAPAN

Japan's east with the huge capital Tokyo is the economic and political centre of the country. The cities of Yokohama and Kawasaki and Chiba prefecture with Narita airport merge seamlessly with the capital.

Almost 40 million people live within a radius of about 50 km/31.1 mi of this megalopolis, the biggest metropolitan region on the planet. A quarter of the island empire's entire population lives and works here. Fortunately, though, there are still a number of natural and cultural oases such as Kamakura, Nikko and the Fuji region. Many visitors only get to experience the central Japanese heartland from the windows of the Shinkansen high-speed trains on the journey to Kyoto. Travelling at 250 km/h (160 mph), they rush past

an apparently endless chain of industrial estates and dreary villages. Away from the track, though, lies the *Ise Grand Shrine*, the heart of Shinto mythology and place of pilgrimage for every Japanese person. Less well-known than Fuji but no less spectacular is the mountain chain that stretches from Nagano to the south-west across the back of the island of Honshu: the Japanese Alps. Mountain-lovers will find twelve 3000-m/9843-ft mountains, deep gorges and impressive landscapes.

HAKONE

(156 C5) (*M G8*) **The fabulous views of majestic Mount Fuji constitute the charm of the tourist stronghold of**

Country of contrasts – hectic and modern in Tokyo, relaxing in the Japanese Alps and historic in Nikko and Kamakura

Hakone (pop. 14,000), although the thermal spas, hiking trails and all sorts of other leisure activities are no less appealing.

One particularly interesting experience is a day trip by the Romance Car of the Odakyu railway from Tokyo-Shinjuku to Hakone-Yumoto *(90 min)*. You can then continue your journey on the Hakone-To-zan train to Gora *(30 min)*. This company also offers the well-priced *Hakone Free Pass* which allows you to use the two lines' trains and buses in one day as well as the Hakone cable car and the pleasure boats *(www.odakyu.jp/english, www.hakone.or.jp)*.

SIGHTSEEING

HAKONE SHRINE

The Hakone-jinja, founded in 757 by Priest Mangan. Its red gate shines over to the lake. The way to the shrine takes you along a cedar-lined shore path *(always open | admission free)* passing by the *Se-ki-sho,* a customs office of the Edo period

Perfect harmony: nothing bothers the Great Buddha of Kamakura

(1600–1868) on the famous *Tokaido*, the Tokyo-Kyoto highway. The rebuilt house next to the customs house is home to a museum on the history of the road. *Daily 9am–5pm, closed 29–31 Dec | Admission 500 ¥ | www.hakonesekisyo.jp/english*

FOOD & DRINK

SOBA SHOP JIHEI

This smart, traditional restaurant on the Hakone-Yumoto shopping street serves soba and udon noodle dishes. The speciality is cold soba with tempura. *Daily while the noodles last | tel. 0460 85 53 54 | Budget*

LEISURE & SPORTS

TOUR OF LAKE ASHI ●

Boats made up to look like pirate ships remind you of Disneyland, and travel daily from Togendai to Hakone and to Moto-Hakone and back. Thanks to the lovely area around Mount Fuji, the trip is very relaxing. *Tours with Hakone Sightseeing Cruise | daily 20 March–30 Nov 9.30am–4pm every 40 min, 1 Dec–19 March 10am–3pm, every 50 min | 970 ¥ for 30 min | www.odakyu.jp/global_site*

WHERE TO STAY

FUJIYA

Japan's first resort hotel (opened in 1878), flagship of the Fujiya chain with charm, traditional and culture in Miyanoshita. Indoor and outdoor pools. *146 rooms | tel. 0460 2 22 11 | www.fujiya hotel.co.jp/en | Moderate*

INFORMATION

HAKONE TOURIST INFORMATION SERVICE

Hakone Town Tourist Association | Yumoto |

tel. 0460 85 57 00 | www.hakone.or.jp/english

KAMAKURA

MAP ON PAGE 158

(157 D5) *(⁄ G8)* **With historic temples, shrines, memorials and buildings and charming hiking trails, this town (pop. 174,000) to the north-west of the Miura peninsula is a pleasant place to visit that is only an hour by train from Tokyo.**

Zen Buddhism first flourished in this former political and military centre of Japan (1192–1333). As well as the numerous temples, the lovely gardens of the *Zuisen-ji* and the *Hokoku-ji* are worth visiting, and it's an easy walk or bike ride there from the station. There are also regular buses along the interesting route to the next railway station at

Kita-Kamakura. Many of the sights are also explained in English.

SIGHTSEEING

DAIBUTSU (GREAT BUDDHA) ★

The famous *Great Buddha* is the town's main attraction. The figure, which stands over 13 m/42.7 ft high, was built in 1252, and was located in a temple hall that fell victim to a tsunami in the year 1495. Today, the Great Buddha sits outdoors, where his calm, balanced radiance can be experienced to full effect. *Daily May–Oct 8am–5.30pm, Nov–April 8am–5pm | Admission 220 ¥ | Enoden train to Hase station*

ENGAKU TEMPLE

Japan's oldest Zen building complex dates back to 1282. *Daily March–Nov 8am–4.30, Dec–Feb 8am–4pm | Admission 300 ¥ | Kita-Kamakura*

★ **Daibutsu (Great Buddha)**
The famous Buddha of Kamakura radiates calm and harmony → p. 43

★ **Ise-jingu**
The national shrine to Shintoism at Nagoya – the buildings are all torn down and rebuilt every 20 years → p. 50

★ **Toshogu**
Wonderful: the mausoleum of the first Great Shogun at Nikko → p. 52

★ **Asakusa Kannon Temple**
Fan along: The incense in this Tokyo shrine is said to protect against accidents and illness → p. 54

★ **Tokyo Sky Tree**
Fabulous views from Tokyo's TV tower → p. 55

★ **Harajuku**
Look out, manga fans: On Sundays this trendy quarter in Tokyo becomes a catwalk for Cosplay fans → p. 56

★ **Meiji Shrine**
Shinto shrine in Tokyo's green lung → p. 57

★ **Odaiba**
'In' quarter in Tokyo on a man-made island → p. 57

★ **Town hall**
All Tokyo is at your feet on the 45th floor → p. 58

★ **Tsukiji Fish Market**
Worth getting up early for: Tokyo's fish market is a feast for all the senses → p. 59

MARCO POLO HIGHLIGHTS

KENCHO TEMPLE

Kencho-ji is the biggest of Kamakura's five Zen temples, and was founded in 1253 by a Chinese priest. *Daily 8.30am–4.30pm | Admission 300 ¥ | Yamanouchi*

TOKEI TEMPLE

Women used to flee to the Tokei-ji, the "Divorce Temple", which was opened in 1285 and is opposite Engaku-ji, when divorce was still the preserve of men. After living here for three years they were considered divorced. *Daily March–Oct 8.30am–5pm, Nov–Feb 8.30am–4pm | Admission 200 ¥ | Kita-Kamakura*

TSURUGAOKA-HACHIMANGU

The town's most important shrine is home to a treasure house with works of art from over 1000 temples in this region. *Daily 6am–9pm | Admission free, museum 200 ¥ | Yukinoshita*

FOOD & DRINK

There is a concentration of good restaurants on the shopping street Komachi-dori as well as on the main road, which runs from the station to Tsurugaoka Hachimangu.

HACHINOKI 🐄

Connoisseurs swear by the kaiseki menus of Buddhist-vegetarian cuisine under this historic roof. *Daily 10am–6pm | At entrance to Kencho-ji | tel. 0467 23 37 23 | www.hachinoki.co.jp | Moderate*

RAITAI

Traditional restaurant in the suburb Takasago in the mountains to the west of Kamakura. It is essential to book in advance. *Daily 11am–7pm | tel. 0467 32 56 56 | Budget*

LEISURE & SPORTS

BEACH LIFE

In summer, people from Tokyo and tourists love the region as a beach paradise. Several broad beaches, mostly volcanic ash, are perfect for swimming and water sports. More and more beach houses have showers and serve snacks. The beaches at Yuigahama, Zaimokuza and Koshigo are popular and easy to get to *(July/Aug)*.

WHERE TO STAY

KAMAKURA PRINCE HOTEL ☆

This hotel is on the popular beach of Shirigahama, and has a golf course and seasonal outdoor pool. Lovely panoramic views of the Pacific. *95 rooms | tel. 0467 32 11 11 | www.princehotels.com | Moderate*

INFORMATION

TOURIST INFORMATION CENTER

You can hire bicycles next to the Information Centre. *Main station | tel. 0467 22 33 50 | en.kamakura-info.jp*

KANAZAWA

(150 B3) (Ø F7) The long journey to the Japanese sea is rewarded with views of well-preserved Samurai houses and fabulous Kenroku Garden – one of the three loveliest parks in the country.

The journey from Tokyo to the harbour town and administrative centre (pop. 450,000) takes only 2½ hours by Shinkansen. A day is probably enough to see all the sights.

SIGHTSEEING

KENROKU GARDEN

Kenroku is best translated as "Six

Attributes Garden". This is a reference to the classic criteria of a Chinese garden: spaciousness, seclusion, artifice, antiquity, waterways and panoramas. At the end of the man-made pond is a stone lantern that is famous for its legs.

6pm, 16 Oct–Feb 8am–5pm | Admission 310 ¥ | Marunouchi

SAMURAI QUARTER NAGAMACHI

The narrow street with earth walls, wooden houses, paper windows and

Tranquil Kenroku Garden: one of the three loveliest gardens in the country

Originally, Kenroku was the garden of Kanazawa Castle, the ruins of which are best avoided because coach-loads of Japanese tourists descend on this popular location for TV dramas involving Samurai. The park was constantly expanded throughout the 17th century. With its 12,000 trees it has been open to the public since 1871. It is an absolute delight to walk through – especially at cherry blossom time, when it is simply teeming with crowds of people. Visitors at the early opening hours *(April–Aug daily 4am–6.45am, Nov–Feb 6am–7.45am, March and Sep/Oct 5am–6.45am | Admission free)* will almost have the park to themselves. *March–15 Oct daily 7am–*

hidden gardens is one of the best-preserved Samurai quarters of the Edo period. The *Nomura residence (daily 8.30am–4.30pm | Admission 500 ¥)* offers a particularly good insight into the life of the warrior caste. The *Terajima House (Fri–Wed 9am–4pm | admission 300 ¥ including flyer in English)* of 1770 has a peaceful miniature garden. A dish of green tea is served in the tea room for 300 ¥. The *Kaga Yuzen Silk Center (daily 9am–noon, 1pm–5pm | admission 350 ¥)*, a former Samurai residence where silk for the kimonos is now dyed, is well worth a visit. *Bus lines 20, 21, and 22 from the station to the stop at Korinbo, then 10 minutes on foot*

SEISONKAKU

Prince Nariyasu of the Maeda clan built this villa at the south-east of Kenroku Park in 1863 as "retirement" home for his mother. The stylish house with the elegant interior is open to the public today. *Thu–Tue 9am–5pm, closed 29 Dec–2 Jan | Admission 700 ¥ with brochure in English*

FOOD & DRINK

KOTOBUKIYA

Very nice restaurant, about 120 years old, north of Oyama Shrine. Dishes are served on elegant Wajima lacquerware. *Daily | Bus stop Owari-cho | tel. 076 2 31 62 45 | www.kanazawa-kotobukiya. com | Moderate*

WHERE TO STAY

NIKKO HOTEL

Large rooms, close to the station and shopping centre. Very good restaurants (Chinese, Japanese). *254 rooms | Honmachi | tel. 076 2 34 11 11 | www.hnkan azawa.co.jp | Moderate*

INFORMATION

TOURIST OFFICE KANAZAWA

At the station | tel. 076 2 32 39 33 | www. kanazawa-tourism.com

WHERE TO GO

WAJIMA (150 B3) (*M F6*)

Although the route is lined with beautifully preserved farms, the only people who come to this tiny place (96 km/59.6 mi from Kanazawa) to the north of the Noto peninsula really love Japanese lacquer work. This craft has been cultivated here for over 500 years, and you can purchase items straight from the artists that are not available anywhere else in Japan. Staff in the tourist office at the station will be pleased to point the way to *Wajima Shikko Kaikan (daily 8.30am–5pm | admission to exhibition 200 ¥),* a type of co-operative. All 68 steps of the lacquer process are explained on the top floor. On the ground floor, the biggest shop of its kind offers top-quality items for any taste and (almost) any wallet. More lacquerware is available at the *Urushi Art Museum (daily 9am–4.30pm | admission 600 ¥).* The *Kiriko Kaikan (daily 8am–5pm | admission 600 ¥)* has huge floats decorated with lacquer art. There is one direct fast train a day from Kanazawa *(135 min).*

NAGANO

(150 C3) (*M F7*) **The industrial town (pop. 383,000) is a famous winter sports centre, and hosted the Winter Olympics in 1998.**

Even though most of the sports facilities have been abandoned and the town is buried in debt, there was something good about the whole business: the motorway from Tokyo and Osaka/Kyoto was extended from the Japanese Alps to here and the section for the Hokuriku-Shinkansen constructed, which halved the travel time from Tokyo to Nagano. Today, more than 4 million visitors come here every year, mainly to ski but also to see one of Japan's loveliest temples.

SIGHTSEEING

ZENKO TEMPLE

This 7th-century temple is bathed in legends. But no one can explain where the *Ikko Sanzon* – the first statue of Buddha, which presumably arrived in Japan from Korea in 552 – has disappeared to. It has supposedly been hidden. A copy may be seen every six years; the next time is 2021. The site was often destroyed by fire, but sufficient donations were received to rebuild it, to a greater or lesser extent. What is now the main hall *(Hondo)* dates back to 1707, and is a listed National Treasure. There is a staircase into the dark at the back. You can feel the way with your hands until you touch something metal – doing so said to secure your entry into paradise. Another attraction is the morning service *Ojuzu Chodai* at 5.30am at which worshippers are blessed with Buddhist prayer beads. *Daily 5.30am–4.30pm | Admission 500 ¥ | 1.5 km/0.8 mi from the station at the northern end of Chuo-dori | Buses every 10 min from the observation deck 150 ¥, taxi about 900 ¥*

FOOD & DRINK

CHIKUFU-DO
Snack bar that serves delicious regional specialities with water chestnuts. *Daily 8am–7pm | Near the main post office | tel. 0262 47 25 69 | Budget*

SUKI-TEI
Best sukiyaki restaurant with top-quality beef. As is the local custom, the animals are fed on apples. *Tue–Sun | Tsumashina | tel. 0262 34 11 23 | Moderate*

WHERE TO STAY

JAL-HOTEL NAGANO
High standard for the price of a business hotel, including lovely views of the Alps. *242 rooms | tel. 026 2 25 11 31 | Toigoshomachi | www.jalhotel.com/nagano | Moderate*

HOTEL KOKUSEI 21
Ultra-modern hotel, also extremely popular with foreigners, in an ideal location with eight restaurants and extensive services. *149 rooms | Agata | tel. 026 2 34 11 11 | www.kokusei21.co.jp | Budget*

INFORMATION

NAGANO CITY TOURIST INFORMATION CENTER
JR station | tel. 026 2 26 56 26 | www. nagano-cvb.or.jp

Pretty colour contrast: black Matsumoto-jo Castle against the autumn leaves

WHERE TO GO

MATSUMOTO (150 C4) *(ⅉ F7)*
This gateway to the Japanese Alps (71 km/44.1 mi south-west of Nagano) is worth visiting just for its lovely castle

Unesco World Heritage Site: farmhouses with thatched roofs in Shirakawa-go

– especially at cherry blossom time (mid-April) and for the autumn leaves (early November). Apart from that, this former base of the Ogasawara clan of the 14th and 15th centuries is now a little sleepy, and a typical Japanese small town with its population of 200,000. The landmark is INSIDER TIP *Matsumoto-jo Castle*, which the locals nicknamed "Crow Castle" for its black façade. It is one of the loveliest and best preserved castles and, which is rare, it was built on a plain and not on a mountain. *Daily 8.30am–5pm, closed 29 Dec–3 Jan | Admission 610 ¥ including Museum of Popular Art | Town centre (15 min on foot from station, bus to Shiyakusho-ame 200 ¥)*

INSIDER TIP *Marumo Ryokan* offers well-priced accommodation in a converted warehouse with shared bathrooms and WC. *8 rooms | tel. 0263 32 0115 | Reservations: marumo_ryokan@ybb.ne.jp | Budget*

SHIRAKAWA-GO (150 B4) (*M F7*)

The historic villages in the river valley of the Shogawa (pop. approx. 1700, 275 km/171 mi from Nagano) are Unesco World Heritage Sites, and accordingly well visited. The large, thatched farmhouses in the Gassho-zukuri style with roof angles of up to 60° are architecturally exceptional. They are designed to cope with the region's heavy snowfalls. The unique constructions look like folded hands. The best views are from Ogimachi-joseki. A convenient starting point is Ogimachi with 110 Gassho residences and the tourist information office *(www.shirakawa-go.org)*. You can also spend the night in some of these traditional buildings *(reservations: info@shirakawa.go.jp)*.

TAKAYEMA (150 B4) (*M F7*)

With its traditional pubs, sake breweries and pretty shops, this little town (pop. 96,000, 18 km/11.2 mi from Nagano) in the Japanese Alps has retained more of its original charm than the oversized rest of the Pacific empire – even if the old town is overrun with tourists. A quarter with three streets – Ichino-machi, Nino-machi and Sanno-machi – with pretty, old craft workshops (in particular carpenters and woodcutters), merchants' houses made of wood, galleries, museums, restaurants and ryokans starts just beyond the river Miya. About 20 minutes from the centre is the Museum Village *(daily 8.30am–5pm | Admission 700 ¥)* with over 30 buildings in the historic Hida style. Everyday objects used by the mountain and farming villages are on display in these houses with the famous steep thatched roofs. The atmospheric,

250-year-old INSIDER TIP *Susaki* (daily 11.30am–2pm and 5pm–9pm | tel. 0577 32 00 23 | *Expensive*) serves exquisite *bonzen* cuisine (cold dishes), and there is a lovely garden for the tea ceremony. The traditional INSIDER TIP *Ryokan Asunaro Hotel* (18 rooms | tel. 0577 33 55 51 | www.yado-asunaro.com/english | *Moderate*) is in an excellent location, and has a garden, top-class kitchen and free WiFi. *Information: Takayama Tourist Information Center | Outside the station | tel. 0577 32 53 28 | www.takayama-guide. com, www.hida.jp/english*

NAGOYA

(150 B4–5) (*M F8*) **Nagoya, home to the vast Toyota group, is the hub of the Japanese automotive industry – and a city with a population of 2.2 million.**
There isn't much of historical interest to see. The proud castle alone is the only trace left of the three most important heroes of Japan's feudal age – Oda Nobunaga, Toyotomi Hideyoshi and Tokugawa Ieyasu. However, more than any other event before, the Expo 2005 drew attention to the lovelier sides of this industrial metropolis.

SIGHTSEEING

ATSUTA SHRINE
The Atsuta-jingu dates back to third century, and is one of Japan's most significant religious buildings. It is the repository of one of the three imperial ruling regalia, the sword Kusanagi-no-Tsurugi. According to the legend, it was given to the Tenno along with the other two imperial relics, the jewel and mirror of the sun goddess Amaterasu. Only the emperor and some Shinto priests have the privilege of seeing it. The shrine is open around the clock. Do

CITY WHERE TO START?
Main station: Strictly speaking, the main station is its own city with department stores, boutiques, restaurants, hotels and an observation deck. From the eastern exit, the Sakura-dori heads towards the giant TV tower. You can get to most of the sights by underground (with signs in English).

try the shrine's version of the local speciality, kishimen noodles. *Admission free | tel. 052 6 71 41 51 | www.atsutajingu.or.jp/ en/intro*

NAGOYA CASTLE
The castle, which was built by Shogun Tokugawa Ieyasu in the early 17th century, was destroyed in WWII and rebuilt in reinforced concrete in 1959. It has two eye-catching heavy, dolphin-like creatures – stylised fish with tiger's heads – made of 18-carat gold at the gable ends, copies of which can be found in every souvenir shop in town. *Daily 9am–4.30pm, closed at the end of the year | Admission 500 ¥ | Naka | tel. 052 2 311700*

TOKUGAWA MUSEUM OF ART
The prints, calligraphies, scroll paintings, artistic lacquerware and ceramics once belonged to the Shogun family Tokugawa. Unfortunately, the most valuable items, including the scroll paintings telling the story of 12th century Prince Genji, are locked away, and you will have to contend with a video. Other worthwhile sights are the Tokugawa Garden and exhibits of the No theatre. *Tue–Sun 10am–4.30pm, closed 20 Dec–3 Jan | Admission 1200, garden 300 ¥ | Higashi | tel. 052 9 35 62 62 | www.tokugawa-art-museum.jp*

TOYOTA MUSEUM

This is where the car giant's story began. The company's development, technology and visions are documented on its first premises, where the Toyota founder still made weaving looms. *Tue–Sun 9.30am– 5pm | Admission 500 ¥ | Nagakute | www. tcmit.org*

FOOD & DRINK

IBASHO

This tiny restaurant specialises in a Nagoya version of unagi – grilled eel. The fish is cooked in the soup or with shallots. *Daily | Naka | tel. 052 2413944 | Moderate*

SEKAI NO YAMACHAN

Popular *Izakaya* (pub) near the station. Spicy chicken wings and other snacks served at the bar. *Daily 5pm–11pm | tel. 0525712106 | www.yamachan.co.jp | Budget*

YABATON

Japanese schnitzel restaurant! The misokatsu are ultra delicious. And there's no missing the logo of a pig in an apron. *Tue–Sun | Osu | tel. 052 2528810 | Budget*

LEISURE

AICHI PREFECTURAL GYMNASIUM ●

This venue for concerts, sporting and other events in the grounds of Nagoya Castle also hosts the famous Grand Sumo Tournament *(2nd–4th Sun in July 3pm–7pm | Day ticket 2800–15,000 ¥)*. Small indoor pool *(daily 6pm–8pm | admission 1900 ¥)*, gym *(daily 4pm–8pm | admission 1200 ¥)*. *Naka | tel. 052 9 71 25 16*

JOYJOY ●

Karaoke anytime and anywhere: sing along in the numerous bars of in the JoyJoy chains, e.g. in Chikusa. Drinks and snacks are also available. *Daily | Admission depending on room, cabin and time from 900 ¥ | tel. 0522490717*

WHERE TO STAY

ANA CROWNE PLAZA GRAND COURT NAGOYA

The no. 1 establishment, 246 modern rooms. Near JR station. Six restaurants, free Internet, gym. *Naka | tel. 052 6834111 | www.anacrowneplaza-nagoya. jp/english | Moderate*

HILTON NAGOYA

Large hotel in a central location, very good service, gym and indoor pool, shuttle service to station and castle. *450 rooms | Naka | tel. 0522121111 | www3.hilton.com | Expensive*

THE WESTIN NAGOYA CASTLE ☆

Nagoya's only hotel with views of the castle. Lovely, quiet area. Excellent value for money. *229 rooms | Nishi | tel. 052 5212121 | www.starwoodhotels.com/ westin | Budget*

INFORMATION

NAGOYA STATION TOURIST INFORMATION CENTER

Central Hall | tel. 0525414301 | www. nagoya-info.jp/en

WHERE TO GO

ISE-JINGU ★ (150 B5) (*Ⓜ F8*)

The 3rd century Shinto shrine, 135 km/ 84 mi south of Nagoya, is one of the biggest in Japan. Every year, 6 million pilgrims come to Ise to see the shrine, a vast complex with two main shrines and a number of secondary ones. Each of the more than 200 buildings is dismantled every 20 years and a new one built on an adjacent site to exacting specifications. The handicraft technology, which has been handed down for millennia, uses no metal nails. On completion, the assigned deity is led to his or her new home in a ritual – *Sengo no Gi*. Western visitors have been allowed to attend this ceremony since 1958.

The main shrine buildings, in particular the inner shrine Naiku, are reserved for the imperial family and high priests. However, most of the ancillary buildings are in the same architecture. The view of the shrine from the path along the western side of the Naiku to the separate shrine Aramatsuri-nomiya 🔆 is almost uninterrupted. On sunny days, the glow of the cypress forest competes with the golden ends of the timber framing. A mirror that belonged to the sun goddess Amaterasu is kept in the Naiku. It is said to be laid on a wooden plinth, wrapped in a brocade bag. Once the bag has become old and brittle, a new one is placed over it without touching the holy mirror. Since this courtly insignia was brought here in the 3rd century, no one has ever set eyes on it. Although the Tenno has the right to see it, it is not known whether he ever exercised it. *Daily from sunrise until sunset | Admission free | Express trains from Nagayo to Ise-Shi or Ujiyamada approx. 1½ hours | www.isejingu.or.jp*

TOBA (150 B5) *(𝑀 F8)*

Toba (150 km/93 mi from Nagoya) is associated with the name Kokichi Mikimoto, who spent his life cultivating natural pearls, which made him a very rich man. In the showrooms, visitors are shown (in English) how the oysters are tricked. To this day, ladies in white garments dive for the pearl oysters, though usually just for show, with a commentary in English. *Observation deck daily 8.30am–5.30pm, winter 9am–4.30pm | Admission 1500 ¥ | Kintetsu line trains from Ise-shi to Toba 20 min.*

Strong women in white garments: the pearl fishers of Toba

NIKKO

🔲 **MAP ON PAGE 159**
(151 D3) *(𝑀 G7)* **"Don't say** *kekko* **(wonderful) until you've seen Nikko!",** **as the Japanese saying has it.**

The admiration is aimed at Japan's most magnificent temple complex and its spectacular surroundings, a valley with beautiful walks. From Tokyo, Nikko (pop.

20,000) is recommended as a day trip by train or bus through an organiser. It can be quiet on weekday mornings, but it's better to avoid weekends and public holidays.

the most exceptional works of art on all the buildings – including the three holy storehouses with carved elephants and the holy stall with the famous three monkeys that "see no evil, speak no evil

One of Japan's most ornate buildings: the Toshogu Shrine in Nikko

SIGHTSEEING

TOSHOGU ★

The most famous sight is the mausoleum of Tokugawa Ieyasu. It was built for the first great Shogun and founder of the Tokugawa dynasty, which ruled Japan over 250 years ago. The shrine complex of exceptional splendour was commissioned by a grandson in 1634, and built over the course of two years by 15,000 craftsmen and the best artists of the day. The complex deliberately reflects the wealth and power of the Tokugawa clan.

The way to the shrine area goes past the holy Shinkyo Bridge, up many stone steps and through a vast gateway beside which is a pagoda. You will find

and hear no evil". The most ornate part of the complex is the "Sunlight Gate" *Yomei-mon*, which is decorated with millions of pieces of gold foil and valuable carvings. *Daily April–Oct 8am–5pm, Nov–March 8am–4pm | Admission 1000–1300 ¥, depending on ticket | Tobu bus from station to Shinkyo or Nishi-sando stops | www.toshogu.jp*

FOOD & DRINK

HIPPARI DAKO

Tiny yakitori and noodle restaurant (three tables) on the main way to the Toshogu Shrine. Extremely popular with foreigners. English menu. *Daily 11am–8pm | Kamihatsuishi | tel. 0288 53 29 33 | Budget*

WHERE TO STAY

NIKKO KANAYA HOTEL
Classic, somewhat conservative establishment with good service, opened in 1873. Perfect for Nikko Park, 30 min by car to the waterfalls. *70 rooms | Kamihatsuishi | tel. 0288 54 00 01 | www.kanaya hotel.co.jp | Moderate*

INFORMATION

Tourist Information | Tobu Nikko station | tel. 0288 53 45 11 | www.nikko-jp.org/ english

WHERE TO GO

LAKE CHUZENJI/KEGON WATERFALLS
(151 D3) (*ØØ G7*)
A drive to the wonderful location of Lake Chuzenji in the Nikko National Park 30 km/18.6 mi from Nikko includes plenty of countryside. The height of the Kegon Waterfalls is up to 97 m/318.2 ft. Mount Nantai-san (2484 m/8150 ft) towers over the lake, while the extinct volcano is a popular destination for hikers. A path to the top leads through the gateway to a shrine that is open from May to October. *To the lake: Tobu bus to the Chuzenji-ko-Onsen stop*

TOKYO

MAP INSIDE BACK COVER
(151 D4) (*ØØ G7*) **Big, bigger, Tokyo: home to almost 9 million people; almost 35 million have settled in the metropolitan region around the city. Outcome: everything happens at the same time. And the future is already happening today.**

Tokyo – skyscrapers reflecting the sky. Multi-lane highways with XXL-sized neon

WHERE TO START?
Shinjuku station (U B5) (*ØØ b5*): The biggest traffic hub in the city is the perfect starting point for a visit to Tokyo. This is the intersection of the ● Yamanote circular railway, which is ideal for a round trip, most suburban trains and the perfect underground network that will take you to the 23 boroughs and almost all the sights with ease.

signs. Shopping malls in pink and glitter. And endless crowds of people who seem to come from all over.

The skyline of all this consists of around 100 skyscrapers in the centre. First the 42-floor Atago towers shook up the city centre, then along came another highlight in the Roppongi Hill complex with a 54-storey office tower, cinemas and lots of shops. After that, midtown flourished as an elegant city in the city, and the rather wild Shiodome complex that developed into vast New Tokyo on the 76.6 ac of the former goods station. Despite the latent risk of earthquakes and the devastation of 11 March 2011 that also shook the metropolis and caused the skyscrapers to sway threateningly, Tokyo continues to shine with ever-new architectural tops. The skyscrapers around the station in the central district Marunouchi and the Tokyo Sky Tree, at 634 m/2080 ft the new landmark of the Japanese metropolis, soar up out of one of the world's most hyperactive skylines. Tokyo is currently preparing for the 2020 Summer Olympic Games (*24 July–9 Aug*) with construction and infrastructure projects.

Tokyo's 23 boroughs can be reached from virtually anywhere thanks to its perfect subway system. For basic orientation: the rich and sparkling Japan can be

The Tokyo Sky Tree reaches high into the sky above the roofs of the Asakusa Kannon Temple

found between the imperial palace and Ginza; the young and fresh version in Shibuya, the best temples and the Tokyo Sky Tree landmark are in Asakusa. Odaiba is the place for relaxation.

SIGHTSEEING

ASAKUSA (U F1) (*f1*)

Even if the ultra-modern TV tower dominates this quarter on the Sumida River today, its many shopping streets, pubs and restaurants, and craft businesses will give you a good idea of what pre-modern Tokyo used to look like. Asakusa (pronounced Assacksa) was once famous as a nightclub district with houses of pleasure, theatres and fairgrounds. Later on, it was where the first western opera was performed, the first cinema film shown – and where the first striptease club opened. Asakusa's centre is *Sensoji,* better known as the ★ *Asakusa Kannon Temple.* The

way to it passes through the "Thunder Gate" *(Kaminari-Mon)* with one of Tokyo's best-known photographic motifs, a 3.3 m/10.8 ft high lantern that weighs 100 kg/220 lb. The gateway is a copy, but the heads of the statues of the gods Thunder and Wind are old. The *Nakamise-dori* with its many souvenir shops goes straight to the main temple, past a large incense holder. Devoted believers wave the smoke of the glimmering sticks in front of their faces: it is said to offer protection against disease and other hardships.

A golden shrine in the temple is said to contain a golden image of the goddess of mercy, Sho Kannon. According to legend, in 628 the figure was found by two fishermen close to the river estuary, who then went on to found the temple. The large hall *Kannon-do* was destroyed several times, but rebuilt in 1958. Many Japanese come here to pray for good fortune after putting money in a box. In addition to the many small halls – the *Awashima-do,* for instance, is dedicated to the well-being of women – the 48 m/ 157.5 ft high five-storey pagoda catches the eye; like the large hall, it is one of Japan's National Treasures *(visits to main building daily 6.30am–5pm | asakusa-nakamise.jp/e-index.html).*

The *Asakusa Shrine,* which was built in the Edo period, is open all year round. The Sanya-Matsuri shrine festival is one of Tokyo's most spectacular and most popular folk festivals. It takes place every year in the middle of May.

The famous architect Kengo Kuma cleverly clad the new *Asakusa Centre of Culture and Tourism (daily 9am–8pm, lookout until 10pm | admission free | www.city.taito.lg.jp)* in wood, which is extremely effective. Its eight storeys look like loosely stacked boxes. It is directly opposite the Kaminari-Mon gateway, with a café, exhibition rooms, tourists' lounge (free public computers), counters (information/tickets) and an ✁ observation deck on the 8th floor with views of the Tokyo Sky Tree and the Nakamise-Dori. The replica of the *Nihonbashi Bridge* at the entrance holds pride of place, but the other reproductions from Tokyo's history are equally effective and well worth seeing. The *Edo Tokyo Museum (Tue–Sun 9.30am–5.30pm, Sat 9.30am–7.30pm | admission 600 ¥)* shows the ascent of the Japanese metropolis from the Shogun rule to modern Tokyo.

The ★ *Tokyo Sky Tree (daily 8am–10pm | day ticket first observation deck 2000 ¥, second observation deck plus 1000 ¥ | www.tokyo-skytree.jp/en)* soars 634 m/ 2080 ft into the sky. Its ✁ observation decks at 350 m/1148 ft and 450 m/ 1476 ft are great attractions. At the foot of the 9.1-ac complex are 310 shops and restaurants, a planetarium and an aquarium.

Incidentally, ● at the weekends, residents of Asakusa give visitors free guided tours of their quarter *(Sat/Sun 11am and 1.15pm | SGG (Systematized Goodwill Guide) | Contact: Asakusa Culture Tourist Information Center | tel. 03 62 80 67 10).*

GINZA (U E4) *(∭ e4)*

The famous glittering strip with its many colourful main and side streets is the actual centre of Tokyo. Today, designers and luxury manufacturers, especially foreign ones, try to outdo each other with their fabulous boutiques and equally fabulous prices. However, there are now also department store chains with more modestly priced clothing. Find details of inexpensive hotels, restaurants and other money-saving tips on the website *www.tokyocheapo.com*. After a fire in 1872, the elegant quarter with seven large department stores, lots of restaurants, galleries and shops was rebuilt as the first western-style quarter with

LOW BUDGET

You can spend the whole night at the *Ooedo Onsen Monogatari*, a bathing complex in an old theme park based on "old Tokyo", for just 1480 ¥ – you won't find better-priced "accommodation" anywhere else in Japan. *Daily 11am–9am on the next day, no admission between 7am–11am | admission 1980, after 6pm 1480, 5am– 9am 1380 ¥ | Odaiba | tel. 03 55 00 11 26 | www.ooedoonsen.jp*

Find details of affordable hotels, restaurants, shops and tips for inexpensive events in Tokyo on the website *www.tokyocheapo.com*.

stone buildings and street lights. The *Matsuzakaya* went on to make history as Japan's first department store that no longer required customers to remove their shoes before entering.

HARAJUKU ★ (U A–B4) (*ℳ a–b4*)

This bustling district around the eponymous station is Tokyo's centre of fashion, and accordingly much-loved by its young people. This is also where you will find chic Omotesando alley, also known as "Tokyo's Champs Élysées" because it is where the country's first street cafés opened. In addition to the best-known Japanese fashion labels such as Issey Miyake and Rei Kawakubo, more and more expensive international boutiques and restaurants are opening here. The shops down the side streets, especially on Takeshita-dori, sell zany fashions for Cosplay fans as well, copied outfits and, of course, the music of the Japanese rock and pop scene. On Sunday, the forecourt transforms from a station into the stage for a costume show.

IDEMITSU MUSEUM OF ART (U E4) (*ℳ e4*)

Japanese and Chinese art (porcelain, paintings, calligraphy, bronzes), famous for the ink works by the Zen monk Sengai. *Tue–Thu and Sat/Sun 10am–5pm, Fri 10am–7pm | Admission 1000¥ | Marunouchi | www.idemitsu.com/museum*

IMPERIAL PALACE (KOKYO) (U D3) (*ℳ d3*)

The residence of the Emperor and his family on the site of the former castle is like a vast green island in the middle of the city. The palace is only open to the public twice a year, on 2 January and on the Emperor's birthday on 23 December. However, you can walk through part of the surrounding ● garden. It is particularly

FOR BOOKWORMS AND FILM BUFFS

Rising Sun ... of a Bitch: How the Japanese Drove Me Crazy – Christoph Neumann's book, which was first published in 2006 in Germany (the first English edition dates from 2015), provides an insight into the "naked craziness of daily life in Japan". The German author has been living in Tokyo for many years

South of the Border, West of the Sun – Haruki Murakami, currently Japan's most successful author, dissects the souls of the people of Tokyo. The novel was described as pornographic by some European reviewers – a point of view, which Japan's critics cannot understand

Cherry Blossoms – director Doris Dörrie's 2009 film is about life and death in Japan. She was just as fascinated by Japan's spiritual strength in her earlier works "Enlightenment Guaranteed" and "The Fisherman and his Wife"

Spirited Away – Japan's most successful film to date (2003) is an anime fantasy film. Director and manga artist Hayao Miyazaki won an Oscar (among other awards) for this film. "Spirited Away" tells the story of a little girl who enters the spirit world of myths, ghosts and gods. A kind of unleashed Disneyland, where the one thing you must never do is forget your own name.

lovely in spring, when the cherry blossom and azaleas are out, and in summer for the roses. *Garden Tue–Thu, Sat/Sun 9am–5pm, closed 25 Dec–3 Jan | Admission free | www.kunaicho.go.jp*

MEIJI SHRINE ★ (U A4) (*Ø a4*)

The city's magnificent Shinto Shrine, Meiji-jingu, is in the middle of a 173-ac park. It was built as a memorial to the Meiji emperor (1850–1912), whose rule saw an end to the isolation policy and Japan on the way to becoming a modern state. It was destroyed in WWII, but rebuilt true to the original. The N*i-no-Torii* is the biggest wooden shrine gateway in the country. On New Year's Day, tens of thousands of pilgrims come here to make a donation and pray for good fortune. *Opening hours change monthly, but are usually daily 6am–4pm | Admission free | www.meijijingu.or.jp/english*

ODAIBA ★ (0) (*Ø 0*)

A district that effectively grew up out of nothing, and instantly became trendy for the "in" crowd and for shopping. This ultra-modern quarter started on a man-made island in the Bay of Tokyo in 1996, since then it has shone consistently with new shopping centres and attractions. From the ☼ jetty and the ☼ beach there are lovely views of the Rainbow Bridge and Tokyo. You can spend hours strolling around the shopping, restaurant and entertainment centres and watch (mostly) young Japanese at their leisure activities. The Statue of Liberty and building of the private TV company Fuji are eye-catching. The journey (from JR Shimbashi) on the driverless Yurikamome (laughing lion) lines over Rainbow Bridge is an experience. Close to the end of the Odaiba Bridge are the Museum of the Sea, the massive complex of the Toyota motor company,

Harajuku: trendy quarter for Japan's fashion-conscious youth

and the ● *Ooedo Onsen Monogatari*. There are a total of 16 different pools in the culture and water park with hot natural springs. In the vast complex in the style of a Japanese town from the historic Edo period (1603–1868), you must wear a yukata (a cotton kimono) that is included in the admission (see box p. 55).

INSIDER TIP ▶ RAINBOW BRIDGE (U E6) (*Ø e6*)

An attraction for joggers and walkers: the 798 m/2618 ft long suspension bridge, 60 m/196.9 ft above the sea at its highest point, between Shibaura Pier and Odaiba over Tokyo Bay. Not many people know this: the lower of the two decks is open to pedestrians. On the ☼ Southern Way you'll have wonderful views of the harbour as far as Yokohama, and on clear days as far as Mount Fuji, 90 km/55.9 mi away. The skyline of the mega city to the north looks close enough to touch. One way takes about an hour, and it's not possible to change to the other side of the bridge. Warning: The gates close promptly! *Summer 9am–9pm, winter 10am–6pm*

passengers a day, *Shinjuku* railway station is one of the busiest in the world.

The main sight is the 243 m/797 ft high, 48-storey ⭐ *Town Hall (Tokyo Metropolitan Government Building)*. The people of Tokyo admire the twin-towered complex with the Citizens Plaza built by star architect Kenzo Tange as the "new capital", but equally curse it for a "tax tower" because it cost them 850 million £/1 billion US$. Over 13,000 peo-

Busy street life in the suburb Ueno: it's never still in the Ameya-yokocho Passage

SHINJUKU (U B2–3) (🗺 b2–3)

Shinjuku, "new accommodation", used to be a new-build region outside the town with cheap places to stay and brothels. Shinjuku was not incorporated until 1932, after the station was built and the area became a place of entertainment for Tokyo's less-well-off citizens. During the boom years, West Shinjuku – which now boasted 18 skyscrapers – became the symbol of the economic rise. By contrast, entertainment is the order of the day in the red light district Kabuki and the restaurant alleys. With around 2 million

ple work here. In clear weather, the view from the ● 〰 observation deck on the 45th floor is particularly impressive, and if lucky includes Mount Fuji. *Daily 9.30am–10.30pm, South Observatory 9.30am–5pm, closed at the end of the year | Admission free | www.tokyometro.jp/en*

TOKYO STATION (U E3) (🗺 e3)

In 2007, the capital's central station, the departing point for all Shinkansen trains, was completely converted and rebuilt, and is now flanked by skyscrapers. The heart, the brick building of 1914, has been refurbished, and now once again houses a hotel, a museum, an art gallery and an international tourist centre.

TOKYO NATIONAL MUSEUM OF MODERN ART (U E1) *(ᴍ e1)*

Collection and changing exhibitions of contemporary Japanese art, excellent wood prints, ink drawings and Ikebana. *Tue–Sat 10am–4.30pm | Admission 420 ¥, special exhibitions 900 ¥ | Chiyoda | www. momat.go.jp*

TSUKIJI FISH MARKET ★ (U E5) *(ᴍ e5)*

Chefs, gourmets and tourists all love Tokyo's fish market, which is the biggest in the world. 2400 t of sea creatures are auctioned off here every day, one-third of the country's total production. You'll have to get up early if you want to experience it: the dealers start carting their freight into the auction room at 4.30am. By 5.30am, the more than 400 eateries and shops selling all kinds of fish accessories plus vegetables, fruit, meat and every imaginable household appliance in the area are open. Retailers, housewives and tourists buy until 10am. Warning: The market with the tuna auction *(Inner Market)* moved to Toyosu in November 2016; at the time of going to press it was not known whether the *Outer Market* and its streets and stands would remain here. *Mon/Tue and Thu–Sat 3am–1pm | Chuo | www.tsukiji-market.or.jp*

UENO, UENO PARK (U E1) *(ᴍ e1)*

Japan's first public park *(Keno-koen)* delights with its temples, famous pagoda and most of the capital's museums, and is a complete haven of peace – apart from the boozy sessions at cherry blossom time. The Samurai statue of Saigo Takamori at the southern park entrance,

Kiyomizu-Kannon Temple, said to protect the area against evil spirits, and the museums are all interesting. Something else that is entertaining outside the park is the old `INSIDER TIP` Ameya-yoko-cho passage near Ueno station, which has hundreds of dealers and market criers. *Ueno*

FOOD & DRINK

ANDY'S SHINHINOMOTO (U E4) *(ᴍ e4)*

Rustic Izakaya pub with plenty of atmosphere and a tremendous selection of dishes for sharing. English menu, English-speaking staff. *Daily 5pm–midnight | Yurakucho | tel. 03 32 14 80 21 | Budget*

HINOKIZAKA ⚘ (U C5) *(ᴍ c5)*

Japanese restaurant in the Ritz Carlton with one Michelin star. The Hinokizaka is in Roppongi's midtown complex. The view from the 45th floor is as fabulous as the elegant interior. The Saturday brunch menu serves the "best of Japanese cuisine" on all three counters. *Daily 11.30am–2.30pm and 5.30pm–9.30pm | Akasaka | tel. 03 34 23 80 00 | www.ritz carlton.com | Expensive*

LA BOHÈME (U B4) *(ᴍ b4)*

Branch of the chain that is found all over Tokyo; open 24 hours. Inexpensive pasta with a touch of Japan. *Daily | Jingumae, Jubilee Plaza Building | tel. 03 54 67 56 66 | Budget*

`INSIDER TIP` NEW YORK GRILL ⚘ (U B5) *(ᴍ b5)*

"In" restaurant on the 52nd floor of the Park Hyatt Hotel with fabulous views. International cuisine, quite good prices at lunchtime (book!). *Daily | Nishi-Shinjuku | tel. 03 53 23 34 58 | tokyo.park.hyatt. com | Expensive*

SHABUSEN (U E4) (🗺 e4)

Traditional shabu-shabu restaurant with good prices at lunchtime. *Daily | Ginza-Core Building, 2F | Ginza | tel. 03 35 71 17 17 | Budget*

TAKEYABU (U C5) (🗺 c5)

Tremendous selection of top-quality, hand-made *soba* noodle dishes. Holds one Michelin star. The owner makes his wholegrain buckwheat pasta with spring water from Gunma. Reasonable: the lunchtime menu. *Daily 11.30am–3.30pm and 6pm–9pm | Roppongi Hills Residence B, 3rd floor | Roppongi | tel. 03 57 86 75 00 | Moderate*

TEN-ICHI (U E4) (🗺 e4)

Elegant tempura restaurant with a stylish atmosphere, popular with foreigners. Booking recommended! *Daily | Ginza | tel. 03 35 71 19 49 | Expensive*

INSIDER TIP ▶ TOFUYA-UKAI ● (U D5) (🗺 d5)

Fresh tofu and other specialities. The popular establishment is in a wonderful garden at the bottom of Tokyo Tower. Tradition is important here. Reasonable set lunch. *Daily 11am–8pm | Shiba-koen | tel. 03 34 36 10 28 | www.ukai.co.jp/shiba | Moderate*

TSUKIJI SUSHI-SEI (U E5) (🗺 e5)

Popular sushi restaurant beside the fish market. Also popular with fish traders. *Closed Sun | Tsukiji | tel. 03 35 41 77 20 | Moderate*

SHOPPING

INSIDER TIP ▶ AKIHABARA (U E2) (🗺 e2)

Where has the electronic future already started? The techno-mecca of Akihabara sets the trends. The biggest selection in the world (Electronic Town, Akky, Laox) and lots of little shops with good bargains. A centre for fans of mangas and anime, computer games and Cosplay cafés where the waitresses wear costumes. *Soto-Kanda | Chiyoda*

DIVERCITY TOKYO PLAZA (U F6) (🗺 f6)

Mega department store in Odaiba with 154 shops selling inexpensive fashion and discounted goods. With a currency exchange, bowling alleys, cafés and 🌱 rooftop vegetable garden. The first interactive "Gundam Front Tokyo" is a great attraction for science fiction fans. An 18-m/59.1-ft robot from the anime series "Mobile Suit Gundam" shows what's what on the front of the building. *Daily 10am–9pm, restaurants 11am–11pm | tel. 03 63 80 78 00 | www.divercity tokyo.com/en*

HIKARIE (U A3) (🗺 a3)

Shibuya's new landmark is the 34-storey Hikarie complex right next to Shibuya station; it also has a concert hall, museums and art galleries. The 200 shops are aimed primarily at female shoppers in their late 20s to 40. *Daily 10am–9pm, restaurants 11am–11pm | tel. 03 54 68 58 92 | www.hikarie.jp/en*

ISSEY MIYAKE (U B4) (🗺 b4)

Japan's cult designer for practical, unusual and always fashionable pleated creations. The flagship store in Minami-Aoyama has in abundance what can be difficult to obtain in Germany (but not elsewhere). *Daily 11am–8pm | www.isseymiyake.com*

INSIDER TIP ▶ MIKIMOTO (U E4) (🗺 e4)

Flagship store of the famous Japanese pearl farmer Mikimoto. Pearls in any colour, size and price. *Daily 11am–7pm | www.mikimoto.com*

Techno-mecca Akihabara: the electronic future has already started here

MITSUKOSHI GINZA (U E4) *(ⓜ e4)*

Ginza's landmark, popular meeting place and renowned department store with a INSIDERTIP fabulous food hall. *Daily 10.30am–8pm | Ginza | www.mitsukoshi. co.jp/store*

INSIDERTIP OMOHARA (U B4) *(ⓜ b4)*

Fashion theme park in the fashion mecca Harajuku with 27 shops selling clothes with plenty of high-tech (virtual changing rooms, interactive overview etc.). The dramatic entrance takes you up escalators, up high to the ☕ café with views of the busy, bustling Jingumae intersection. *Daily 11am–9pm, restaurants 8.30am–11pm | Jingumae | tel. 03 34 97 04 18 | omohara.tokyu-plaza.com*

ORIENTAL BAZAAR (U B4) *(ⓜ b4)*

All Japan under one roof. Prints, kimonos, antique Asian furniture, pearls and every imaginable souvenir. *Jingumae | www. orientalbazaar.co.jp*

TOKYO MIDTOWN (U C5) *(ⓜ c5)*

Popular building complex in the Roppongi quarter with bars, boutiques, design centres, cafés, museums, exhibitions, pubs with terraces and a park. *Akasaka, Minatu | www.tokyo-midtown. com/en*

INSIDERTIP UNIQLO (U E4) *(ⓜ e4)*

The flagship of the Japanese textiles group is based over 12 floors in the Ginza with cool, reasonable leisurewear and cosmopolitan staff. *Daily 11am–9pm*

LEISURE & SPORTS

IKEBANA ●

The Japanese work their way up in the art of flower arranging, and reach various levels after years of training. There are taster courses for beginners at the big ikebana schools. Booking in advance is essential. *Sogetsu Ikebana School | Aoyama | tel. 03 34 08 11 51 | www.soget su.or.jp/e*

TEA CEREMONY ●

Chado, the "Way of tea", is an extremely stylish Japanese work of art. Even with no prior knowledge, and without spending hours sitting on the floor, you can experience the special atmosphere of this mindful form of pleasure in a half-hour tea ceremony at the garden restaurant *Happo-en (daily 11am–4pm | Admission with garden from 2000 ¥ | tel. 03 34 43 31 11 | www.happo-en.com/english/garden)*.

ENTERTAINMENT

Anyone who wishes to experience the "real" night-life of Tokyo should go to Roppongi, the city's international pleasure quarter. There are plenty of foreign restaurants and an amazing number of discotheques and bars, also with live music. The *Square Building* houses numerous clubs and discos, including the poplar *Birdland Jazz Club (Roppongi)*. One restaurant with a variety show is the *Kakuwa (Tue–Sun 5.30pm–4am | Admission 20 ¥ | Roppongi | tel. 03 54 14 88 18 | www. kaguwa.com)*. You should absolutely book! The night scene very quickly changes it locations. Latest info: *www. metropopolis.co.jp*.

Foreigners are not exactly welcome at most of the establishments in Tokyo's infamous red light district, *Kabuki-cho*, while they can fall victim to all sorts of cons elsewhere. But it's nevertheless worth taking a stroll through the colourful lanes and alleys.

KABUKI-ZA (U E4) (*Ⓜ e4*) ●

Kabuki theatre has a long tradition in Japan: the plays and dances are staged with lavish costumes and plenty of make-up; all the performers are male. Japan's most famous kabuki theatre reopened in a new building in the old place with the famous façade in 2013. *Chuo | tel. 03 35 41 31 31 | www.shochiku.com*

EMPTY ORCHESTRA

The Japanese deal with stress and shyness at karaoke. Even if it is tricky to match up the chosen playback tune with the displayed text (which is often in English), it doesn't matter – anyone can be a star.

To sing with an "empty orchestra", which is what the term karaoke actually means, preferably head for one of the multistorey karaoke establishments in the *Big Echo* chain. In Ginza in Tokyo, the soundproof cabin costs 700 ¥ per hour/person, 5200 ¥ for a small party, and 9600 ¥ with 20 singers.

At happy hour *(until 6pm)* the unlimited set price is 1200 ¥, and you can sing through from midnight until 5am for 2800 ¥. *Daily | Yurakucho | tel. 03 52 51 51 51 00*

INSIDER TIP **TAKARAZUKA REVUE**
(U D4) *(𝄞 d4)*

Mangas, girls and musicals are performed by women only in this large theatre (2069 seats) – delighting Japanese ladies in particular, who queue for hours for tickets to the premières. The founder decided, in 1914, to start a female counterpart to the "elitist", all-male performers of the kabuki theatre. The actresses, who attend a very hard school, are all stars, the opulent and usually melodramatic shows (on stage stairs with 26 steps) something very special. *Yuraku | tel. 03 52 512001 | www.kageki.hankyu.co.jp/english*

WHERE TO STAY

CONRAD HOTEL ᴽ (U E5) *(𝄞 e5)*
Much-praised hotel in the Hilton Group with two Michelin restaurants and fabulous views of Tokyo Bay. *290 rooms | Higashi-Shimbashi | tel. 03 63 88 8000 | www.conradhotels.com | Expensive*

KATSUTARO-RYOKAN (U E1) *(𝄞 e1)*
Traditional guest house with seven rooms (three without bathrooms) close to Ueno Park. *Taito | tel. 03 38 21 47 89 | www.katsutaro.com | Budget*

KEIO PLAZA INTERCONTINENTAL ᴽ
(U B2) *(𝄞 b2)*
47-storey hotel with fabulous views and 1448 comparatively reasonable deluxe rooms. *Nishi-Shinjuku | tel. 03 33 44 0111 | www.keioplaza.co.jp | Moderate*

PALACE HOTEL ᴽ (U E3) *(𝄞 e3)*
This traditional hotel near the imperial palace is elegant and exclusive since it was reopened as a modern luxury hotel with a gym and pool on the fifth floor and ten restaurants! Fabulous location and views. *290 rooms | Chiyoda | tel. 03 32 115211 | www.palacehotel.co.jp | Expensive*

Legendary: Tokyo Station Hotel

TOKYO STATION HOTEL (U E3) *(𝄞 e3)*
This legendary hotel which is in the Tokyo station complex has reopened in an entirely new look and with three times the rooms. The ᴽ rooms with views of the imperial palace are especially popular. The breakfast room in the 9 m/29.5 ft high atrium is fabulous. *150 rooms | Chiyoda | tel. 03 52 201112 | www.the tokyostationhotel.jp | Expensive*

TOKYO YOYOGI YOUTH HOSTEL
(U A4) *(𝄞 a4)*
This hostel is a reasonably priced accommodation in the old Olympic Village of 1964. *60 rooms (only single rooms) |*

Climbing Mount Fuji is a mass activity: you can't get lost

Yoyogi-kamizono | tel. 03 34 67 91 63 | www.jyh.or.jp | Budget

VILLA FONTAINE HAKOZAKI (U E3) *(🕮 e3)*

Popular with Japanese business travellers and tourists. The hotel offers excellent value for money, and is in a good location in the city centre near the City Air Terminal and underground. *163 rooms | Nihonbashi | tel. 03 36 67 33 30 | www.hvf.jp | Budget*

INFORMATION

TOKYO TOURIST INFORMATION CENTER (U E4) *(🕮 e4)*
Shin Tokyo Building, 1 F | Marunouchi | tel. 03 32 01 33 31 | www.jnto.go.jp

TOURIST INFORMATION (U G7) *(🕮 0)*
Narita Airport, Terminal 1: tel. 0476 30 33 83 | Terminal 2: tel. 0476 30 33 83 | www.narita-airport.jp

WHERE TO GO

FUJI (150 C4) *(🕮 G8)*

The 3776-m-high volcano, 90 km/ 55.9 mi from Tokyo, is venerated as a holy mountain. It is how Japan would like to be perceived: big, even, pure, mystical. Every single Japanese wants to climb to its highest peak at least once. The five Fuji-go-ko lakes at the northern foot of the mountain are lovely mirrors for its sublimity. Prices at the *Youth Hostel Kawaguchiko (11 rooms (communal bathroom) |*

Kawaguchiko | tel. 0555 720630 | Budget), about 8 minutes' walk from the station, are reasonable. To climb Mount Fuji see p. 116.

IZU PENINSULA (150 C5) (*ffl G8*)

Residents of the capital travel to the peninsula some 100 km/62 mi south-west of Tokyo to swim, surf, dive and chill. The landscape, beaches and towns are often picturesque, and the thermal spas are especially popular. The best-known bathing resort is Shimoda, which also has the longest beaches. There are charming views of the Pacific from the ⚘ cliffs of the Southern Cape. The top spot on the somewhat quieter western coast is the ● ⚘ Sawada-koen-Rotem-buro Onsen (Sep–July Wed–Mon 7am–7pm Aug 6am–8pm | Admission 500 ¥ | tel. 0558 52 00 57) in Dogashima. Here, you can relax high up on a boulder with fabulous views of the cliffs.

YOKOHAMA (151 D4) (*ffl G7*)

Tokyo merges seamlessly with Japan's second biggest city. Yokohama's (pop. 3.7 million) position by the sea and the foreign visitors give this harbour town a cosmopolitan openness. The major sights are the harbour with its prome-nade, nearby Chinatown with hundreds of good restaurants and exotic shops, and the new quarter of Minato-Mirai with the Landmark Tower. An elevator travelling at 45 kph/30 mph catapults you to the ⚘ restaurants on the 68th and 70th floors, and the observation deck on the 69th floor (in the Royal Park Hotel | daily Sep–June 10am–9pm, July–Aug 10am–10pm | admission 1000 ¥ | tel. 045 2 211111). The views from the upper storeys are spectacular in all directions.

Calm, elegance and contemplation are the order of the day in the INSIDER TIP Sankei-in garden (daily 9am–4.30pm, closed at the end of the year | admis-sion for the outer and inner gardens 300 ¥ each | bus from Sakura-cho sta-tion to Honmoku), which was created by a wealthy silk merchant in 1906. Surrounded by ponds and flowering vegetation are 16 architectural treas-ures, including a 500-year-old 3-storey pagoda.

RYOKAN

The Japanese say that anyone checking in to these refuges of peace and style is treating themselves to a gentle attack on all the senses. They at least have to accustom themselves to an establishment that lacks anything a western hotel would have – apart from a bathroom: no proper bed, but a mat on the tatami floor. No restaurant, because the standard dinner and breakfast (included in the price) are served in the rooms. No room keys, no numbers; just a sliding door with a Japanese symbol above it. No lobby, no gym, no business centre. Guests are at home in the traditional sense. Ryokan are actually exclusive hotels that date back to the days when even the nobility travelled on foot. The best addresses are therefore to be found on the old imperial road between Tokyo (Edo) and Kyoto, such as the Asa-ba in the Izu National Park (Shuzenji | tel. 05 58 72 70 00).

WESTERN JAPAN

Western Japan is primarily the region around Osaka, Kyoto and Kobe – also known as the Kansai region. The cultural landscape represents the historic rivalry between the Emperor and the Shogun in Kanto.

The people here are considered as efficient as they are hedonistic. Kyoto and Nara, where the emperors resided between 794 and 1886, embody classic Japanese culture. Osaka and Kobe offer modern urban vitality.

HIMEJI

(153 E3) (*Ⓜ E8*) **The main attraction of the town (pop. 536,000) can be seen from the train line.**

The castle, national cultural treasure and Unesco World Heritage Site, is lovingly called *Shirasagi-jo* ("The White Heron Castle") by the Japanese. Himeji is a perfect as a day trip from Kyoto, Osaka or Kobe.

SIGHTSEEING

HIMEJI-JO ★
The "Castle of Castles" is considered the most spectacular fortification and one of the architectural landmarks of Japan. This fascinating building, which is one of Japan's National Treasures, has also been the setting for various Samurai films. The snow-white façade on the hill of Himeji can be seen from the Shinkansen. The 14th century building, also called the

Historic glory in Kyoto and Nara, urbanity in the industrial region Osaka-Kobe – variety is guaranteed here

"White Heron Castle" for its simple beauty, was constantly developed by various royal clans, and completed in its current guise in 1609. Even then, the castle was considered a sensation because it could be seen from a tremendous distance, and the 46 m/151 ft high defence system was extremely well secured.

Like many Japanese castles, it has a "blind storey" on the inside; a floor without a false ceiling that enabled the inhabitants to hide relatively safely when necessary. Following an extensive re-

furbishment, the spacious complex was restored to its former brilliance in 2015. Himeji is full of exciting stories about powerful feudal lords, proud Samurai, a happy princess – and a castle ghost. The servant girl Okiku was accused of breaking ten precious porcelain plates, and was drowned in the castle well as punishment. It is said that on stormy nights, you can hear her counting the plates from the depths of the well. A visit in April is a particular delight, when the more than 1000 cherry trees in the castle

Nippon's loveliest example of the art of castle-building: Himeji-jo

grounds are in flower. *Daily 9am–5pm | Admission 1000 ¥ | www.city.himeji.lg.jp/guide/castle*

HYOGO MUSEUM OF HISTORY
The subject is castle-building all over the world. At 10.30am, 1.30pm and 3.30pm, visitors can be INSIDER TIP photographed dressed as a Samurai or in a court kimono. *Tue–Sun 10am–5pm, closed on the day after a public holiday | Admission 200 ¥ | 5 min north of the castle*

KOKO-EN
Park in the traditional Edo style. This used to be the site of the Samurai residences. The views from the 🍵 tea pavilion – 500 ¥ for a cup – are lovely. *Daily 9am–5pm | on the western moat*

HIMEJI MUSEUM OF LITERATURE
Those who are less interested in the local writers come here for building, located north-west of the castle: architect Tadao Ando is considered one of the masters of modern Japan. *Tue–Sun 10am–5pm | Admission 300 ¥ | Yamanoicho*

FOOD & DRINK

Both Western and Japanese food is available near the station.

FUKUTEI
On the way to the castle, Fukutei serves cold kaiseki meals at reasonable prices with traditional Japanese music playing in the background. Illustrated menu. Extremely popular with locals. *Daily 11.30am–2pm and 5pm–8pm | Kamei | tel. 079 2 22 81 50 | Budget*

WHERE TO STAY

HOTEL NIKKO
Next to the station, 20 min on foot to the castle. Three restaurants, gym and indoor pool. *247 rooms | tel. 0792 22 22 31 | www.jalhotels.com/domestic/kansai/himeji | Moderate*

HOTEL WING INTERNATIONAL HIMEJI
B&B, only 400 m/1312 ft from the castle and 700 m/2297 ft from the station; free Internet access, bikes available to borrow free of charge, laundry, drinks machine, restaurant. *111 rooms | Wata | tel. 079 2 87 2111 | himeji.hotelwingjapan.com | Budget*

INFORMATION

Information centre in the station. *Ground floor to the right of the elevator | tel. 078 287 00 03 | www.himeji-kanko.jp/en*

WHERE TO GO

SHOSHA-ZAN ENGYO-JI
(153 E3) *(ﾉ E8)*
The castle temple, around 8 km/5 mi north-east of the station on Shosha-zan hill, has been a place of pilgrimage for about 1000 years. The eight buildings and seven statues of Buddha are considered an important cultural heritage *(daily 9am–5pm | Temple admission 300 ¥)*. A cable car (from the Shosha stop) makes the ascent easier for pilgrims *(one way 500 ¥, return 900 ¥)*.

HIROSHIMA

(153 D3) *(ﾉ D8)* **At 8.15am on 6 August every year, when the bells have stopped chiming, Hiroshima's mayor lowers a roll of parchment deep into the ground in a sad tradition.**

This document records the names of the people who have died in the past 365 days from the effects of the atomic bomb dropped by the Americans in 1945. Sadly, the figure is still almost 5000 people a year. Today, Hiroshima ("Broad Island") also stands for reducing angst,

---

⭐ **Himeji-jo**
Nippon's largest feudal castle, in Hineji and visible from far away, is often used as a backdrop in films → p. 66

⭐ **Peace Memorial Park**
(Heiwa-koen)
Impressive cemetery park with an eternal flame at the centre of the atomic inferno of Hiroshima → p. 70

⭐ **Miyajima**
Delightful: the "floating" gateway of the Itsukushima Shrine near Hiroshima → p. 72

⭐ **Fushimi Inari Shrine**
10,000 red gates line the way to this shrine in Kyoto → p. 76

⭐ **Kinkaku-ji**
The famous "Golden Pavilion" in Kyoto → p. 79

⭐ **Kiyomizudera**
Man, architecture and nature, united in harmony → p. 79

⭐ **Nijo Castle**
Kyoto's Shogun residence with numerous refinements → p. 81

⭐ **Katsura-rikyu**
The imperial villa at Kyoto is one of the loveliest estates in Japan, with a delightful garden architecture and tea houses → p. 87

⭐ **Todai-ji**
Japan's biggest bronze Buddha awaits you in Nara, in a vast temple complex → p. 91

⭐ **Dotonbori**
This glittering, kitschy, colourful destination is a must for visitors to Osaka → p. 96

MARCO POLO HIGHLIGHTS

HIROSHIMA

the fear of life. The city is no longer stuck in unbounded sorrow. There is little in the lively city, with its shopping arcades and restaurants, to remind us of its tragic history, and today 1.2 million people live here, more than twice as many as before the war. No more than 80,000 of them can remember the morning they call the "bright flash of light".

The city on islands in the Ota-gawa Delta is traversed from east to west by the lively, busy Aioiri-dori with the main tram lines from the station. At the western end is the Peace Memorial Park with the A-Bomb Dome. To the south is the Boulevard Heiwa-Odori. In between is the covered shopping and restaurant arcade Hon-dori.

LOW BUDGET

The tourist offices in the major towns and cities will help to find Goodwill Guides. These are locals who guide tourists round the town, and will sometimes also help to find accommodation. They require only to be reimbursed their travel expenses, admission charges and the (shared) lunch. Please arrange at least one week in advance. *Japan National Tourism Organization (JNTO) | Chiyoda | tel. 03 32 01 33 31 | www.jnto.go.jp*

The *Osaka Unlimited Pass* gives you free admission to 24 sights and free travel of public transport, including harbour tours. *Cost: 2000 ¥ for 1 day or 2700 ¥ for 2 days. Available from the Osaka Information Centre Namba | Midosuji Grand Building 1st floor | Chuo-ku | tel. 06 62 11 35 51*

A-BOMB DOME
After controversial discussions, the skeleton of the former Chamber of Industry and Commerce has been declared a Unesco World Heritage Site. This is the very spot where the first atomic bomb used for war purposes exploded on 6 August 1945. The ruins have been preserved. On the eve of the anniversary of the catastrophe, the townspeople set paper lanterns with lit candles in the Ota River. They float towards the sea, in memory of the deceased of each family. *Naka*

PEACE MEMORIAL MUSEUM
The building is called the "Peace Memorial Museum" so as not to antagonise American visitors. It shows the history of the bomb being dropped and records the consequences of the explosion. The guestbook is well worth reading. One American visitor wrote in memory of Japan's war guilt: "Never another Hiroshima! Yes, wholeheartedly. But never another Pearl Harbour, either." *Daily May–Nov 8.30am–6pm, Dec–April 8.30am–5pm | Admission 50 ¥ | Naka*

PEACE MEMORIAL PARK (HEIWA-KOEN) ★ ●
This former banking centre was the hypocentre of the explosion. The main memorial is the cenotaph, an empty tomb with a gabled roof. Its eternal flame is to burn until the last atomic weapon on the planet has been abolished. The words on the memorial to the 200,000 people who died read: "Rest in peace, for the error shall not be repeated." *Naka*

CHILDREN'S MEMORIAL
This moving monument was inspired by the struggle for survival of Sadako Sasaki (1943–1955). The little girl, who

was contaminated radioactively, wanted to make 1000 colourful origami cranes, the symbol of a long life and happiness. Sasaki died of leukaemia when she had finished 663 of them – a victim of the atomic bomb. People from all over the country completed the 1000 cranes, and decorated her grave with them. This became a permanent movement in Japan's schools, and every year the Park of Peace is decorated by millions of origami cranes. *Naka*

FOOD & DRINK

Hiroshima's cuisine specialises in seafood, especially oysters. *Okonomi-yaki* are as famous as they are simple: pancakes with seafood and vegetables.

KANAWA
Boat restaurant with a wide range of oyster dishes: baked, grilled, boiled ... *Daily | Naka | Quay E near the Park of Peace | tel. 082 2 41 74 16 | www.kanawa. co.jp | Moderate*

OKONOMIMURA
Complex with 25 restaurants in the Shintenchi Plaza Building behind the Parco department store. Speciality: okonomi-yaki. *Daily | Naka | tel. 082 2 41 22 10 | Budget*

WHERE TO STAY

ANA CROWN PLAZA HIROSHIMA HOTEL
Hiroshima's best-known hotel is on the Heiwa-O-Dori, which goes to the Park of Peace. *409 rooms | Naka | tel. 082 2 41 11 11 | www.anacrowneplaza-hiroshi ma.jp | Moderate*

HOTEL GRANVIA HIROSHIMA
This modern business hotel is very close

Memorial in steel and crumbling concrete: hiroshima's a-bomb dome

to the station. *410 rooms | Minami | tel. 082 2 62 11 11 | www.hgh.co.jp | Moderate*

RIHGA ROYAL HOTEL HIROSHIMA
On 35 floors in the city's tallest building, and its landmark. *491 rooms | Naka | tel. 082 5 02 11 21 | www.rihga.com/hiroshi ma | Moderate*

INFORMATION

HIROSHIMA TOURIST INFORMATION CENTER
JR Hiroshima Station, on the Shinkansen side | tel. 082 2 61 18 77 | www.hiroshima- navi.or.jp/en

KOBE

WHERE TO GO

MIYAJIMA ⭐ (153 D3) *(⚏ C8)*
The shrine island, 27 km/16.8 mi from Hiroshima, is – along with Matsushima Bay and the Amanohashidate sandbar – one of the "Three Views of Japan".
Miyajima is famous for the red *torii* – gate – in the water. This wooden gate is the most frequently photographed landmark in Japan. It symbolises the entrance to the *Itsukushima* shrine on the island. Probably built in the 6th century, the shrine was built like a jetty into the water. The "Morning prayer room" Asazaya, the left hand of the arched bridge, houses a *treasury (daily 8am–5pm | admission 300 ¥)* with weapons, masks and costumes. One famous postcard motif is the floating *No stage (shrine open daily from 6.30am until sunset | admission 500 ¥ with treasury)* of 1568, the oldest in Japan.

The island with its other sights and restaurants is easy to explore on foot – it's a pleasant half-day excursion from Hiroshima *(ferry terminal to Miyajima near Miyajima-guchi station (Sanyo line), 25 min from main station), also direct from the city centre (70 min to Hiroden-Miyashima station).*

KOBE

(153 E–F3) *(⚏ E8)* **On 17 January 1995, Kobe fell victim to a devastating earthquake.**
6430 people died, 300,000 were left homeless. It was the worst natural catastrophe since the Tokyo earthquake of 1923, and caused a tremendous amount of damage. But today, Kobe has been completely rebuilt, and is a cosmopolitan, trade-oriented, busy harbour city with a popular of 1.5 million. Despite its

The shrine island Miyajima at cherry blossom time: one of the "Three Views of Japan"

economic significance, the harbour city in the Bay of Osaka is of a manageable size. Most of the sights and restaurants are within walking distance of the train stations – the main ones are the Shinkansen station Shin-Kobe and Sannomiya (centre of the city). It will take you 20 minutes to walk from one to the other, but you can also take the underground *(ticket 200 ¥ | 2 min)*

SIGHTSEEING

CHINATOWN
The tiny quarter of Nankinmachi, a typical Chinese settlement, is particularly charming in the evenings, with its delightfully colourful façades and the red lanterns of the restaurants. The 40,000 Chinese who live in Kobe are not the only ones who like coming here. *5-minute walk south of the Motomachi city train station*

KITANO
Wealthy merchants and foreign diplomats had this exclusive residential area *(Ijinkan)* built at the beginning of the Meiji period (1868–1912), when Kobe became an important commercial harbour. The Japanese appreciate the Western way of life, and love to stroll along its tiny streets. Over 20 of the mostly Victorian-style residences, some of which are extremely impressive, are open to the public, some free of charge. Most of the bars, pubs and hostels are in Kitano.

ROKKO CABLE CAR
This cable car runs from the OPA shopping centre near Shin-Kobe station up to the 400-metre ⋇ Rokko ridge, from where you have fabulous views of the town and the bay of the inland sea, especially at sunset. *Cable car winter daily 9.30am–5.30pm, spring and autumn*

9.30am–8pm, otherwise 9pm | one way 550 ¥, including return 1000 ¥

FOOD & DRINK

Kobe is famous for its particularly tender, extremely expensive beef. It is also an excellent destination for Indian and Arabic food.

INSIDER TIP GANKO SUSHI
Kobe's branch of the popular Ganko chain welcomes you in a pleasant atmosphere and an English menu with delicious, reasonably-priced sushi and other specialities. Recommended: the set lunches (until 5pm). *Daily 11.30am–11pm | tel. 078 3 6 12 1 34 | Moderate*

INSIDER TIP KOBE PLAIRSIR
One good place near the main station to sample the famous Kobe beef *(Wagyu)* at reasonable prices. The lunch is particularly good value. You can also watch the chefs at work. *Daily 11.30am–3pm, 5pm–10.30pm | tel. 0785 71 01 41 | www. kobe-plaisir.jp | Moderate*

MORIYA HONTEN
Traditional restaurant in the city centre that serves reasonably priced special Kobe beef (teppanyaki). *Opening hours vary | Chuo | tel. 078 3 9 14 3 06 | www. mouriya.co.jp/en | Moderate*

WHERE TO STAY

KOBE MERIKEN PARK ORIENTAL HOTEL ⋇
Large modern hotel right by the harbour with an indoor pool, five restaurants, harbour and mountain views, free shuttle bus to Sannomiya station. *319 rooms | tel. 078 3 25 8 1 11 | Chuo | www.kobe-orientalhotel.co.jp/english | Moderate*

TOYOKO INN KOBE SANNOMIYA NO. 2
Popular B&B in the TI chain. Good location in the city. Free Internet, laundry, drinks machine, microwave. *334 rooms | tel. 078 2 32 10 45 | Chuo | www.toyoko-inn.com | Budget*

INFORMATION

In Sannomiya station | tel. 078 3 22 02 20 | feel-kobe.jp/_en

KYOTO

 MAP ON PAGE 159
(153 F3) (*Ⓜ E8*) **"I want to see dusk over Kyoto from Kiyomizudera. And the sky over Nishiyama, as the sun sets behind it." The writer Yasunari Kawabata (1899–1972) wrote a literary memorial to the city in his novel "Kyoto".** He could not speak highly enough of the view of the lovely old imperial residence from the "Temple of Clear Water". His suicide spared the poet from having to see his "beloved" lose her elegant looks. Kyoto (pop. 1.5 million) has recently experienced a tremendous building boom. Every year it attracts 30 million tourists who may bring plenty of money with them, but also cause traffic jams, overfill the car parks, are noisy and leave vast quantities of rubbish.

Kyoto's beauty needs to be discovered. None the less, though, the ancient imperial metropolis has over 17 Unesco World Heritage Sites – 13 Buddhist temples, three Shinto shrines and the Shogun castle, all of which are open to the public. Highlights such as the old emperor's palace, Nijo castle, the Golden and Silver Pavilions are like oases. The Kamo River divides the city into west and east, Gojo Avenue into north and south. Most of the temples and gardens are

CITY WHERE TO START?
The old imperial metropolis was Japan's first city in a chequerboard layout, which makes orientation much easier. To the south, the main station is the best starting point for trips. You'll find most of the highlights in **Higa-shiyama** to the east. The north has stone gardens and the Golden and Silver Pavilions, while to the west is the template complex of **Arashiyama**. The modern Kyoto is embedded in the centre.

there, within walking distance of the city perimeter. This applies above all in the east (from the south): Sanjusangendo, Kiyomizudera, Gion, Maruyama Park, Chion-in, the Heian Shrine, Nanzenji (from there along the philosopher's path Tetsugaku-no-michi to the Ginkakuji), north-west to Ryoanji and Ninnaji. Two-hour (approximately) INSIDER TIP guided tours of Gion in English *(March–Nov, Mon, Wed, Fri 6pm–7.40pm, Dec–Feb, Mon, Wed, Fri 5pm–6.40pm | 1000 ¥ per person | www.waraido.com/walking/gion.html)* introduce you to the former geisha quarter.

SIGHTSEEING

BOTANIC GARDEN
An oasis on the Kamo River. 12,000 different plant species thrive on 59.5 ac. The park was created in 1924, and is particularly special at cherry blossom time. Many people come here from Kyoto for picnics. *Daily 9am–4pm | Admission 200 ¥, greenhouse plus 200 ¥ | Sakyo*

CHION-IN
Although not everything in Japan's most

extensive temple complex is old – most of the buildings date back to the 17th century – it is the biggest. At 24 m/78.7 ft, the two-storey main gate San-mon is the tallest in the land. And south-east of the temple is Japan's biggest bell. It was

DAIGO-JI

The Buddhist temple in Fushimi to the south-east was founded on Mount Daiho in 874, destroyed repeatedly and extended. The highlights are the five-storey pagoda of 951, one of the oldest build-

The Buddhist temple complex of Daigo-ji is in the middle of a fabulous garden

cast in 1633, weighs 74 t, and it takes the strength of 17 monks to strike.

The vast main hall from the 17th century is dominated by the golden altar and an image of sect founder Honen. The hall is connected to the Dai Hoko meeting hall by the famous "nightingale" floor: the wooden boards were built with metal ends so that every step creates a piercing sound – to protect against unwanted intruders. *Daily March–Sep, 9am–4pm, Oct–Feb, 9am–3.30pm | Admission free, 500 ¥ for the Hojo and Yuzen gardens | Higashiyama*

ings in Japan, and the Sampo-in with impressive murals. Another highlight is the wonderful garden of Sanpoin Teien, which was extended in 1598 for the cherry blossom parties of the famous warrior Toyotomi Hideyoshi, and is considered a prime example of luxurious Momoyama architecture. The complex consists of the upper and lower Daigo, which are connected by a path that is very steep in places. The sporty ascent, which is followed by many pilgrims, takes a little under an hour, and passes numerous shrines and temples. *Daily 9am–4pm | Admission to garden, pagoda/hall and museum 600 ¥ each | Fushimi | www.daigoji.or.jp*

DAIMONJI-YAMA ☼

Look east, and you can see the character *dai* on the side of this mountain from almost everywhere. Every year on 16 August, huge fires are lit on the mountains in order to guide the souls of the dead to their families – one of the most impor-

The way is the destination: gateway of some 10,000 red *torij* to the Fushimi Inari shrine

tant rituals in the Obon festival. Those who don't mind the 5-km/3.1-mi ascent *(just behind Ginkaku-ji)* will be rewarded by wonderful panoramic views.

DAITOKU-JI

This temple complex in north-west Kyoto is an important centre of the Zen school Rinzai. Visitors can visit eight of the 24 temples, including the venerable main temple of Daitokuji. This is where image of the tea master Sen no Rikyu is kept, and many Japanese worship it almost

like a relic. The master, who was apparently forced to commit ritual suicide by the Shogun in 1591, is a symbol of purity. However, the best-known temple is the Daisen-in, famed for its Zen garden. The stone and gravel path can be followed from the terrace. It is not necessary to fall into a deep meditation to appreciate the perfect composition of spirit and nature. The small garden Koto-in is a must in autumn, when the maple trees drop their deep red leaves over old moss. INSIDER TIP Be sure to come in the morning, as the light is perfect then for wonderful photos. *Koto-in: daily 9am–4pm (closed on a number of random days), Daisen-in: 9am–4.30pm | admission 400 ¥ to each*

FUSHIMI INARI SHRINE ★

This shrine in the south, well-known for its apparently endless gateway, is a visual, spiritual and sporting experience. Around 10,000 red torii line the path to the peak of Mount Inari, which is reached via a path more than 4 km/ 2.5 mi long, and quite steep in places. The gates, all of which have been donated, create highly photogenic tunnels in the gentle curves. On the highly recommended ascent, you will see the five shrines of this vast complex as well as numerous stone sculptures of foxes – the fox is considered the earthly messenger of the god of the harvest and of trade. The shrine draws millions of Japanese pilgrims over the two weeks of New Year to pray and make donations for wealth and material success. Thus, Fushimi has the second-highest collect after Tokyo's Meiji shrine. Fushimi, which was founded in the 8th century, is one of the oldest, best-known and most frequently visited shrines in Japan, and the main shrine of the approximately 30,000 Inari shrines. Best time for photos: between 7am and 9am in summer. *Sunrise to sunset | Admission free | Fushimi*

GINKAKU-JI

Built at the end of the 15th century by a Shogun as an elegant villa and secret refuge, the "Silver Pavilion" was intended to be covered in silver leaf. Although this didn't happen, this garden and temple complex is one of the loveliest spots to visit in classic Kyoto. *Daily 8.30am–5pm, Dec–mid-March 9am–4.30pm | Admission 500 ¥ | Sakyo*

GION

Time seems to stand still in some parts of this geisha district. Come around 10 or 11 in the morning, and with a little luck you will see a geisha or a *maiko* whoosh past. On warm summer evenings, shamisen sounds and cheerful singing penetrate the bamboo curtains of the old tea houses (which sadly may not be entered

without prior notification). *North and south of the Shijo-dori on the eastern bank of the Kamo River*

GOSHO (OLD IMPERIAL PALACE)

It might not be the loveliest sight, but because it is so difficult for the Japanese to access, it is very special to them. The complex, which measures 25 ac, became the Emperor's official residence in 1331 and was completely rebuilt following a number of fires in 1855. Its former function ceased in 1868, when the Emperor relocated to Tokyo. Nowhere else in Kyoto has courtly form been as important as it is here, to this day. For instance, the southern gate remains reserved for the Tenno, the eastern gate for the Empress and her mother. Protocol determines how state guests are treated. Presidents go with the Tenno. With regard to female state guests, the preference is to withdraw from the whole affair, to the extent that they are driven through the visitors' gate to the west.

A guided tour (50 min) takes in the Shishin Hall, the "Little Palace" Ko Gosho, the main palace Tsune Gosho and the pond garden O-ike-niwa of the 18 buildings. The buildings are not usually entered. The coronation takes place in the Shinsin-den. It contains the imperial throne under a canopy with a phoenix, with two frames for the Imperial Regalia in front. The Ko Gosho contains three smaller audience rooms with views of the landscaped garden. Views by permission only; contact the office at court *(Imperial Household Agency, through the northwest gate, then right | tel. 075 2 11 12 15 | passport required)*. Foreign visitors will usually be given an appointment immediately for the same day *(application at: sankan.kunaicho.go.jp/order)*. The park to the north of the palace with lots of old cherry trees is open all the time. *Closed*

28 Dec–4 Jan., tours in English Mon–Fri 10am and 2pm, Sat 10am | Admission free | Kamigyo

HEIAN SHRINE

The orange replica of the Emperor's palace of the art-loving Heian Period was constructed in the year 1885 to mark the 1100th anniversary of the city of Kyoto. Walk through the red Otomon gate, and you will come to the large Daigokuden state hall, to the east and west main halls and to the pagodas. Behind is a large pond garden with – unlike the evergreen Zen gardens – trees that blossom with the seasons. The eye-catcher is a Chinese-style wooden bridge combined with a pavilion, as was customary for every elegant villa during the Heian period as an observation platform for watching ornamental fish. And so the golden age of Japan's former nobility lives on, symbolically, in this garden. *Daily 6am–5.30pm (seasonally 6am–5pm), garden daily 8.30am–5pm (seasonally 8.30am–4.30pm) | Admission free, garden 600 ¥ | Sakyo*

HONGAN-JI ●

Eastern Temple (Higashi Hongan-ji): Even though this massive building 500 m/ 1640 ft north of the main station was rebuilt with little artistic appeal after a major fire in 1895, it still has one highlight: a rope that was woven from the hair of female followers of the Buddhist school of Jodo Shinshu – "True Pure Land Buddhism" – that was used to procure wood for the new construction. *Daily 6am–5pm (occasionally longer in summer and on feast days) | Admission free | Shimogyo | www.higashihonganji.or.jp*
Western Temple (Nishi Hongan-ji): To the people of Kyoto, it is clear that this temple 400 m/1312 ft west of the Eastern Temple is the more important one, because they

usually tend to omit the direction Nish (west) automatically from its name. It is the main home of the Buddhist school Jodo Shinshu, which has more than 12 million followers and 10,000 temples all over the world. The complex, which was built by Hideyoshi Toyotomi starting in 1591, also has much to offer architecturally. The five buildings that make up the complex are included in the loveliest constructions of the Azuchi Momoyama period (1568–1600). The marvellous main hall is open again, and the fabulous pictures, woodwork and metal decorations in the Daisho-in hall are also all worth a visit. The sliding doors were all made by masters of the Kano School. The rooms are named after the particular motif in the art. The "Stork Chamber" was the Shogun's counselling room. Also preserved is the state hall of Fushimi Palace, where the ruler used to bathe, drink tea and then rest. *Daily 6.20am–4.30pm, occasionally longer depending on the season | Admission free | www.hongwanji. or.jp/english*

KINKAKU-JI ⭐

The most frequently photographed building in Kyoto is the "Golden Pavilion". And indeed, the walls of the top two floors of this three-storey house are covered in gold leaf. It was built at the end of the 14th century as the retirement residence for a Shogun who then decided to become a monk at the age of 37. On clear days, the building is reflected in the waters of the garden lake, creating an unbeatable composition of blue, gold and green. It is particularly attractive when it has snowed, but also when the leaves turn in autumn and the rich shades of red enhance the colourplay. *Daily 9am–5pm | Admission 400 ¥ | Kita*

KIYOMIZUDERA ⭐ ●

Very early in the morning, old Kyoto still ticks the way it did 1000 years ago. Before classes of noisy schoolchildren descend on the Kiyomizu Temple, founded in 798, the wooden floors on the terrace of the famous prayer house in the old imperial city creak, the scent of incense fills the air, and monks are lost in silent prayer. The harmony between man, architecture and nature is exceptional when the maple trees turn deep red at the end of November, creating the frame for the prettiest view of Kyoto. The name "Pure Water Temple" is a reference to the spring under the main hall. Those seeking healing scoop up the water in long ladles and pour it over their hands. The wooden terrace, supported by hundreds of pillars, is one of Japan's landmarks. Jumping from this ledge is a metaphor in Japanese for "daring to do something difficult".

People who arrive early can walk along the so-called teapot paths almost without interruption – paths that lead to the temple and where (in addition to the obligatory kitsch) the best pottery in Kyoto can be bought. The flag stoned streets INSIDER TIP *Sannenzaka* ("Slope of Three Years") and the adjoining *Ninenzaka* ("Slope of Two Years") that branch off are the perfect spot for a cup of green tea and happy dreams of old Japan. *Daily*

When the maple turns deep red it's time to visit Kiyomizudera

6am–6pm | Admission 300 ¥ | Higashiyama | www.kiyomizudera.or.jp

INSIDER TIP KYOTO INTERNATIONAL MANGA MUSEUM ●

Japan's first museum devoted to the entire spectrum of manga culture, opened in 2007. This joint project between the

Salted vegetables: speciality on Nishiki market

city and Seika University, which has a separate faculty for manga, carries approximately 300,000 exhibits. It has the first issues of Japanese mangas from the early Meiji period (1868–1912) and a number of foreign versions. Visitors have access to around 40,000 volumes from all periods. *Tue–Thu, 11am–6pm | Admission 800 ¥ | Karasuma-dori, Nakagyo | www.kyotomm.com*

KYOTO STATION

The avant-garde main station in central Kyoto is a masterpiece of transportation technology, although its architectural attributes are a matter of some dispute. The building complex with a department store, hotel, shopping and restaurant arcades has been the subject of much debate. Many citizens consider the construction an irritant that does not go with the style or character of the city. At the heart of the futuristic construction of steel and glass is an atrium measuring 60 m/196.9 ft in height and 500 m/1640 ft in length. On the 14th floor is an ☼ observation deck, and the Tourist Centre is located on the second floor *Kyo-navi (daily 8.30am–7pm).*

KYOTO TOWER ☼

Directly opposite the station is Kyoto Tower, visible from afar, and resembling a Japanese candle. This is a good place to get an overview of the city when you arrive. The 131 m/430 ft high tower is an excellent aid to orientation. *Daily 9am–9pm | Admission 770 ¥*

MARUYAMA-PARK

This park is a refuge in the busy city, if not exactly a haven of peace. There are old cherry trees all the way up the mountain. The restaurant on the pond *(Budget)* is a romantic photo motif as well as a source of traditional cuisine. The Yasaka Shrine to the south-east of the park is a popular destination for the first visit to the shrine on New Year's Eve or the morning of New Year's Day. On the lovely path to Kiyomizu Temple, sports students from Kyoto offer rickshaw rides with information *(30 min 5000 ¥ per person, 8000 ¥ for two; 1 hr 9000 ¥ per person, 15,000 ¥ for two | Higashiyama). Daily | Admission free | Near the Shijo-dori*

NANZEN-JI

The imperial retirement residence was converted into one of Kyoto's loveliest Zen temples at the end of the 13th century, and today is the main base of the influential Rinzai School. You can enjoy first-class tea in the temple hall while you admire the classic "Leaping Tiger Garden". There are fabulous views of the city from ⚘ the second floor of the vast entrance gate San-mon. Highly recommended: INSIDER TIP▶ *Tenju-an* temple – for its lovely garden. *Admission to temple complex free, main building and other temples 300–500 ¥ | nanzenji.com*

NATIONAL MUSEUM KYOTO

This renowned museum has one of the oldest and most significant collections of Japanese and Asian art. The treasures are presented most impressively in a newly-built, state-of-the-art modern building. *Tue–Sun 9.30am–6pm | Admission 520 ¥ | Higashiyama | www.kyohaku.go.jp/eng*

NATIONAL MUSEUM OF MODERN ART

Known for its collection of contemporary Japanese ceramics and paintings. Changing exhibitions. *Tue–Sun 9.30am–5pm | Admission 900 ¥, special exhibitions extra | Sakyo | www.momak.go.jp*

NIHO CASTLE ⭐

The logic of power dictates that the Shogun's seat should not be far from the palace. Early in the 17th century, Tokugawa Ieyasu had this magnificent complex built in order to show the Tenno who really controlled the empire. However, the famous warrior was obviously not quite so certain of his popularity, and he had the residential tracts fitted with convoluted safety devices. The most famous of them is the "nightingale floor": no one could enter the room without causing the wooden floor to squeak. Bodyguards waited for intruders in secret chambers. Only members of the nobility who submitted to the Shogun were permitted to pass through the large gateway *(Karamon)* and enter the five buildings of the Ninomaru wing. Today, the screens in the fourth chamber *(Ohiroma Yon-no-ma)* and the palace gardens, which were created by the landscape architect and tea master Kobori, are the main sources of interest. *Daily 8.45am–5pm, entry until 4pm, closed 26 Dec–4 Jan | Admission 600 ¥ | Nakagyo*

NINNA-JI

Do not be put off by the dark shapes of the wooden figures that guard the wooden gate: tourists may pass through without hindrance. The complex, which was completed in 888, was originally intended to be used as a palace, but in fact it was only rarely occupied by an imperial prince. It burnt down several times, was made smaller, and is today the main temple of the Buddhist Omura School. The building dates back to the 17th century, and the five-floor pagoda of 1630 is considered a masterpiece of Japanese religious architecture. *Daily 9am–4.30pm | Admission to palace 500 ¥, with an extra charge for the other buildings | Ukyo*

NISHIKI MARKET ●

This market in the middle of the city, which has been in existence for over 400 years, is both an institution and an attraction. There are more than 130 stands and shops selling local specialities. Why not try some of the different foods and culinary creations that are typical of Kyoto's famous cuisines! The variety, range and friendliness of the sellers in the covered hall are impressive and a joy. *Daily from 9am are until approx. 5pm*

RYOAN-JI

Every child in Japan knows the famous Zen garden of the Rinzai School in the north because a visit there is on every school's curriculum. Those who wish to penetrate the mystical conceptual world of the 15 apparently randomly scattered rocks on the carefully barren terrain should be sure to arrive as soon as the gate opens. The garden was created in 1450, but no one knows by whom or what statement it was meant to make. It is up to the individual visitors to decide the secrets of this garden design for themselves. *Daily March–Nov 8am–5pm, Dec–Feb 8.30am–4.30pm | Admission 500 ¥ | Ukyo | www.ryoanji.jp*

SANJUSANGEN-DO

The name of this temple, which was built in 1164 by Emperor Goshirakawa and rebuilt just like the original in 1266 after a fire, means "Hall with thirty-three spaces between columns". The high building is as long as you would expect. Inside are the Thousand Armed Statues of Kannon, the Buddhist goddess of mercy and compassion. The dominating image is a thousand-armed Senju Kannon in the middle, flanked on each side by 500 of the other figures. In fact, there are only 40 arms. However, according to the Buddhist idea, each of the Kannon's arms saves 25 worlds, adding up to 1000.

The Toshiya Festival takes place here every year on 15 January, a traditional archery exhibition contest for which the archers aim through the hall from the gallery on the west side. The idea, which dates back to the Edo period (1600–1868), was that in order to test the competence and military strength of the archers, they had to shoot as many arrows as possible to the other end of the hall. The record of 8000 reaching the north wall was set in 1686. *1 April–15 Nov daily 8am–5pm, 16 Nov–March 9am–4pm | Admission 600 ¥ | 15 min walk east of the main station*

TETSUGAKU-NO-MICHI

The "Philosopher's Walk" is a pedestrian path between Ginkaku-ji in the north and Nanzen-ji in the south, and Kyoto's first place for cherry blossom. A number of famous artists and scientists live in the surrounding area.

TO-JI

Although the temple complex (794) was built to protect the town, the town expanded so quickly that the project soon lost any military value. So the Emperor gave it to the priest Kukai, who founded the Buddhist Shingon School there. Most of the preserved buildings date back to the 17th century. The 21 esoteric images in the Kondo reading hall and in the main hall of the Medicine Buddha Yakushi and his two companions are of artistic significance.

The importance of the five-storey pagoda, which was rebuilt five times over the course of the centuries, is instantly obvious. At a height of 57 m/187 ft, the current building of 1643 was not only the biggest pagoda in Japan, but for a long time also the maximum building height in Kyoto. *Daily 8.30am–4.30pm | Admission 500 ¥ | approx. 15 min walk south of the main station*

FOOD & DRINK

Kyo-ryori, the local version of kaiseki cuisine, is famous. It is served cold. A simple meals costs 6000 ¥, a full-course menu between 15,000 and 50,000 ¥.

INSIDER TIP **AJIRO**

Award-winning vegan Zen cuisine with

first-class tofu specialities at the south-ern exit of Myoshin Temple. *Fri–Tue 11am–9pm | Ukyo | tel. 075 4 63 02 21 | Moderate*

C. COQUET
Popular Internet café with free ac-cess with every order. *Fri–Wed 11am–8pm | Corner Teramachi and Maru-tamachi, near the Imperial Palace | tel. 075 2 12 08 82 | www.cafe-ccoquet. com | Budget*

HONKE OWARIYA
People have been happily "slurping" here for generations: Kyoto's oldest noo-dle restaurant at the centre of the city near Nijo Castle has been an institution for 540 years, especially its soba soups. Detailed menu in English. *Daily 11am–7pm | Nakagyo | tel. 075 2 31 34 46 | www. honke-owariya.co.jp/english | Budget*

KITCHO ☂
Delightful location in the hills of Arashija-ma: one of the most expensive, but also the best restaurants in Japan. *Thu–Tue (by reservation only) | tel. 075 8 8 111 01 | www.kitcho.com/kyoto/shoplist_en/ arashiyama | Expensive*

MANKAMERO
The imperial court used to dine at this wonderful building with the fabulous garden. It still serves the very finest aris-tocratic cuisine today – at the appropri-ate prices. It is essential that you book. *Tue–Sun 5pm–11pm | Kamigyo | tel. 075 4 41 50 20 | Expensive*

OKUTAN
Kyoto is famous for tofu, and this is one of the best addresses for these special-ities. It only serves set tofu meals. *Fri–Wed 11am–4pm | Higashiyama | tel. 075 7 71 87 09 | Moderate*

TADGS BAR
International meeting place with Happy Hour. *Daily 11.30am–11pm | Kiyamachi | tel. 075 2 13 02 14 | www.tadgs.com | Budget*

Exclusive restaurants: Kyoto is famous for its excellent cuisine

SHOPPING

Nowhere else in Japan will you find such a broad range of old artwork (geisha dolls, lacquerware, silk weaving, and woodcuts). The biggest selection is at the *Kyoto Craft Center (daily 10am–7pm | Sakyo | tel. 075 7 61 70 00)* and the *Kyoto Handicraft Center (daily 10am–7pm | Ku-mano Jinja Higashi, north of the Heian Shrine)*.

On the 21st of every month, the *To-ji* is the venue for the *Kobo-san flea market*. Whether you're looking for a kimono belt or a kettle, you're sure to strike gold here – and at reasonable prices. It's not unusual for genuine – to a greater or lesser extent – antiques to be found.

The tour is unique, but at 50,000 ¥ it's also expensive. *Tel. 075 5 41 12 34 | www. kyoto.regency.hyatt.com*

Dance of the cherry blossom: trainee geisha performing at the Gion Kobu-Kaburenjo

Shinmonzen-dori: Street of antique shops with small pieces of furniture, ceramics, scrolls and woodcuts at hefty prices. *North-west of Maruyama Park*

AUTHENTIC CRAFTS

Emperors and aristocrats preferred silks from Nishijin and today exclusive boutiques all over the world buy the *Hosoo Kyoto* company's brocades to decorate their luxury stores. The "Authentic Tour" offered by the *Hyatt Regency* hotel in Kyoto with a private chauffeur and English interpreter, features this and other traditional workshops that make works of art out of bamboo, wire mesh, pewter and wood. The masters themselves guide visitors through their workshops.

LEISURE & SPORTS

JAPANESE COOKING

Emi Hirayama shows you in her own kitchen how a housewife from Kyoto cooks – from typical and very healthy dishes, including vegetarian ones, to the famous sweets from the former royal seat. And as an added bonus, you also learn a lot about the city and its inhabitants. *From 4500 ¥ | Duration approx. 3 hrs | Booking essential at www.kyotouzuki.com*

ENTERTAINMENT

At cherry blossom time in spring and when the leaves turn in autumn, many of the temples open their gardens in the evening with festive lighting. The spectacle, which is much criticised by protectors of the environment, is lovely to look at but also a tremendous waste of energy. And more importantly, the spotlights scorch the leaves, even causing the death of some old trees. Dates available from the tourist information centres.

GION CORNER
Geishas and the art of entertainment: presenting the tea ceremony, ikebana, courtly music and dance. Perhaps a little touristy, but also a good insight. *Daily 7.40pm and 8.40pm, no performances on 16 Aug or Nov–Dec | Admission 3150 ¥, tickets available in many hotels | Higashiyama | tel. 075 5 611119 | www.kyoto-gioncorner.com*

GION KOBU-KABURENJO ●
Maikos (trainee geishas) perform the traditional cherry blossom dances *(Miyako o dori)* here in April. The performances (three day) are a cultural highlight. *Yaei Kaikan | Higashiyama | tel. 075 5 611115*

INSIDER TIP MINAMI-ZA
One of the oldest Kabuki theatres in Japan. English translation on headsets. The highlight is the Kaomise Festival from 1 to 26 December, when the cream of Japan's dramatic art meet on the stage. Booking essential! The admission price varies, depending on the time of day and performance. *Shijo-dori | Higashiyama | tel. 075 5 611155*

PONTO
The modern entertainment mile used to be the place of execution in Kyoto and today, as the world of the "little man", is the counterpart to the elegant Gion. On the banks of the Kamo are numerous restaurants serving traditional Japanese food, but also a modern, western-orientated experimental cuisine. Not to be missed on summer evenings: a drink in one of the INSIDER TIP terraced bars above the river. *Hankyu S train to Kawaramachi*

WHERE TO STAY

ECO+TEC KYOTO
Reasonably priced accommodation in a very good location, ideal for staying several days. No restaurant or breakfast, but lots of free offers: coffee, tea, water, Internet, microwave, two massage chairs, computer access, two uses each of washing machine and tumbler (detergent 50 ¥). Towels, bed linen, cleaning by agreement, bicycle hire *22 rooms | Higashiyama | tel. 075 5 33 10 01 | www.ecoandtec.jp/en | Budget*

HYATT REGENCY KYOTO
Charmingly rebuilt house in the style of a ryokan. Short walk to Sanjusangen-do and Kiyomizudera. Excellent Japanese and western cuisine. *189 rooms | Higashiyama | tel. 075 5 4112 34 | www.kyoto.regency.hyatt.com | Moderate*

JAM HOSTEL
In an excellent location in the middle of the city near the Kamo River and Gion: reasonably priced hostel with 20 beds in five rooms, including two separate rooms. With a sake bar and café. *Tel. 075 2 0133 74 | www.jamhostel.com | Budget*

KYOTO BRIGHTON HOTEL
Hotel with a pretty atrium, quiet location west of the imperial palace. French gourmet restaurant. *183 rooms | Kamiyagi | tel. 075 4 4144 11 | www.brightonhotels.co.jp/kyoto | Expensive*

SUPER HOTEL KYOTO SHIJYO KARAWAMACHI

Excellent value for money, small rooms, mini bathroom, but perfectly functional. Good breakfast, free wi-fi in the lobby and free onsen. Central location in Nakagyo. *177 rooms | tel. 075 2 55 90 00 | www.superhoteljapan.com/en | Budget*

WESTIN MIYAKO

The "grand dame" is blossoming under new management. Great location in the hills near Nanzen-ji. *528 rooms | Higashiyama | tel. 075 7 71 71 11 | www.starwood hotels.com/westin/property | Moderate*

YACHIYO RYOKAN

Elegant guesthouse near the Nazen-ji Temple in the north-east. Atmosphere, design, garden, food – all first-class. The staff are excellent, the communal bath a dream. Expensive, but not as much as the smart hotels in the city. Free Internet. *17 rooms | tel. 075 7 71 41 48 | Higashiyama | www.ryokan-yachiyo.com | Expensive*

INSIDER TIP YISHIKAWA INN ●

An oasis in the middle of the city: fabulous little ryokan in the traditional sukiya style with a garden and a famous tempura restaurant. Food and service are excellent. *8 rooms/suites | Nakagyo | tel. 075 2 21 68 05 | www.kyoto-yoshikawa. co.jp | Expensive*

INFORMATION

TOURIST INFORMATION CENTER

Main station | tel. 075 3 43 05 48 | www. pref.kyoto.jp/visitkyoto/en

WHERE TO GO

ARASHIYAMA (153 F3) (*Ø E8*)

Togetsu-kyo Bridge on the western edge of the city is a popular destination at cherry blossom time. Lovely: watching the cormorant fishermen on a summer evening walk. Romantic: when the river banks glow red and orange from the autumn foliage. Too busy at weekends! The *Tenryu-ji* temple complex is only a few hundred metres from the north shore of the Hozu River. It is said that a priest once saw a dragon rise up out of the river here in a dream. The "Temple of the Dragon Sky" was built in 1339 out of concern that this could represent an imminent upset on the part of the Emperor. This vast complex with 150 sub-temples contains two landscaping highlights: *Sogenchi Garden*, which was created in the 14th century, and what is probably the loveliest and most magnificent *tea house* in Kyoto in the *Okochi-Sanso Garden*. The architect altered the hill in the background to resemble a particular mountain in China that was greatly admired by the Japanese nobility.

The aristocratic writers in old Japan knew where to go for the best inspiration. The poet Fujiwara Teika (1162–1241), famous for his anthology of Heian-era poetry, resided right behind the temple on Mount Ogura, which still offers a wonderful ☼ Kyoto panorama today. Even the ten-minute walk through a dense and mysterious bamboo forest is an experience. *Daily April–Oct 8.30am–5.30pm, Nov–March 8.30am–5pm | Admission 900 ¥ including a cup of green tea and confectionery | City train Keifuku Arashiyama to Hankyu Arashiyama, from Kyoto station by train to JR Saga, 15-minute walk to Arashiyama*

BYODO-IN (153 F3) (*Ø E8*)

Ideally, the temple should be seen from a bird's-eye view. When it was converted in 1052 from a stately villa belong to the Fujiwara clan into a Buddhist site, the architects wanted to make a memorial to the phoenix in Chinese mythology that was honoured in ancient Japan as a protector of Buddha. So they built the Phoenix Hall, which has two bronze birds on the roof. It is not instantly obvious, though, that the central hall with the three corridors that represent the wings and tail resemble a phoenix landing on the lake. *Daily 8.30am–5.30pm | Admission 600 ¥, 300 ¥ for the Phoenix Hall | JR-Nara train to Uji (approx. 40 min)*

ENRYAKU-JI (150 A5) (*M E8*)

The famous, vast monastery on Mount Hiei near Otsu (15 km/9.3 mi from Kyoto) has a varied history and many famous alumni. Founded in 788, the priests, who had close links to the imperial court, were said to have built 3000 sub-temples, maintained their own army of warrior monks and interfered heavily in political power struggles. Because the influential congregation made a pact with his enemies, in 1571 warlord Oda Nobunaga had all of the monks in the monastery slaughtered and most of the buildings burnt down. Today, only three pagodas and around 120 temples remain. The complex is divided into three different areas: *Todo* (East Pagoda), *Saito* (West Pagoda) and *Yokawa*. The main sights are in the Todo region, where most of the buildings are to be found including the main and Amida halls, which was added in 1937. It is a pleasant walk to the Saito side. Yokawa is 4 km/2.5 mi away, and not quite so interesting. *March–Nov 8.30am–4.30pm, Dec 9am–4pm, Jan/Feb 9am–4.30pm | Admission 700 ¥ (for all three regions), treasury 500 ¥*

KATSURA-RIKYU ★ (153 F3) (*M E8*)

The Emperor's summer seat is one of the loveliest estates in Japan. The little palace was built in 1624, and the elaborate landscaping and scattered tea houses are among the cream of Japan's classical building culture. It is said that

Bridges through an enchanting bamboo grove in arashiyama

the garden designer Kobori accepted the contract under three conditions: firstly, no limit on costs; secondly, no deadline for completion; and thirdly, no visits from the client for the duration of the work. The entire complex apparently only offers front views. Little gardens with paths of river gravel and mossy stones are grouped around the pond. The landscape designers provided hundreds of different perspectives. The visitor entrance is the *Miyuki Gate*, which was erected in 1658.

Inside the garden are three offset buildings – *Furu-shoin* has a lovely terrace for moon-viewing, while *Naka-shoin* houses valuable paintings and *Miyuki-den* was reserved for visits by the emperor. Visits only by confirmed booking (only possible from Japan; major hotels can arrange one for the same day). *Mon–Fri | Katsura | sankan.kunaicho.go.jp | Hankyu city train to Katsura*

KITAYAMA MOUNTAINS
(153 F3) (*Ⓜ E8*)

The Northern Mountains are a popular retreat for the people of Kyoto. They used to be a refuge for people who were banished from the imperial court, who would flee there. Today, the mountainous landscape is much visited in summer in particular because it is cooler than in Kyoto. The region is known for its lovely hiking trails, numerous old temples and onsen baths. The open yuka restaurants on platforms above the Kibune River offer refreshment. From rurally idyllic *Ohara (1hr by bus from Kyoto)* there is a 3.5-km/2.2-mi footpath from the Jakko-in temple complex to the famous vast *Sanzen-in (daily 8.30am–4.30pm | admission 700 ¥),* that includes several small temples, shops and restaurants. The Buddhist temple Sanzen-in, which is off the beaten tourist track, was founded in 804. Its picturesque garden is extremely impressive, especially in the morning and in snow. It can get very busy in autumn, though, for the foliage.

Charming paths lead from *Takao* to the north-west of Kyoto *(approx. 1hr by bus)* through forests and three temples. The loveliest is said to be *Jingo-ji (daily 9am–4pm | admission 500 ¥)* with a long stairway to the main gate and the Golden Hall.

INSIDER TIP SAIHO-JI (KOKE-DERA), JIZO-IN (153 F3) (*Ⓜ E8*)

The "Moss Temple" (*Koke-dera),* first mentioned in 731, is a rare masterpiece of ancient Japanese landscaping. Today's site consists of a Zen stone garden of 1339 and an even older landscape design with a lake in the shape of the symbol for "heart". A hundred different types of moss are believed to grow in this part of the garden (although experts can only confirm 30 to 40). In order to preserve the beauty and idyll of the site, only a maximum of 200 people are allowed to enter every day. The concierge of a good hotel can take care of the advance booking for you *(the Kyoto Hotel is recommended | tel. 075 2115111).* Punctuality is expected, as is a donation of 3000 ¥. The 90-minute tour is preceded by a period of Zen meditation or other compulsory religious programme. *Nishikyo*

NARA

MAP ON PAGE 158

(153 F3) (*Ⓜ E8*) **Where to get a welcome from a real messenger of the gods? Around 1200 tame deer roam the city park of the imperial metropolis Nara (pop. 370,000).**

In pre-Buddhist times, the animals were considered "Messengers of the Gods", and hunting them was a capital offence. Today they are considered a "Living National Treasure".

Thanks to its excellent climate, Japan's first permanent capital would probably have remained the Tenno seat for a long time – had it not been for the monks. After the priest Dokyo seduced an empress, and thus almost managed to seize the throne, the court decided to put an end to the growing influence of the clergy and founded a new residence in Kyoto, 50 km/31.1 mi away. This meant that the Nara period lasted only 75 years.

However, the foundation stone for an independent Japanese culture was laid under Chinese influence. Buddhism advanced to become the state religion, and largely shaped the country's social and artistic life – which is still evident today in its buildings and images.

The city at the northern end of the fertile Yamato valley celebrated its 1300th anniversary in 2010. The city park *Narakoen* is in the eastern part of the old imperial seat, which is within walking distance of the central station Kintetsu. The JR station is a little further west from the city centre, but you can also walk to the main sights from there. You can also hire a bike and explore the city.

SIGHTSEEING

HEIJO IMPERIAL PALACE

From 710 until 784 Heijo Palace, as the centre of the ancient capital Heijo-kyo, was arranged in a square. After the relocation of the metropolis, the buildings and temples on the 320-ac complex fell into disrepair. In 1955 the administration started archaeological excavations and the first restorations. To mark the 1300th anniversary, the large Audience Hall and East Palace Garden were reconstructed and a museum of history opened. *Replica of Heijo Palace: Tue–Sun 9am–4pm | Admission free | Heijokyo Museum of History: Tue–Sun 9am–4pm | Admission free for foreigners (present passport), otherwise 500 ¥ | both Sadaiji*

Also known as the Shrine of 10,000 Lanterns: Kasuga Taisha

ISUI GARDEN

This is probably the loveliest garden in Nara and, with a carp pond from the Meiji period (1868–1912), is a welcome oasis for relaxing after a strenuous tour of the temples. For 450 ¥, you can enjoy the view over a cup of tea. *Wed–Mon 9.30am–4.30pm | Admission 900 ¥ | Mima*

Great Buddha in the Todai-ji: the right hand represents peace

KASUGA TAISHA

The attraction of the clan shrine of the Fujiwara, which was founded in the 8th century, is the lantern path with 3000 stone and bronze lanterns. Twice a year, they are lit at 6pm for the Mantoro Lantern Festival (*2–4 Feb, 14–15 Aug*), followed the next day by a traditional dance performance in the Apple Garden. The insignia used in the Shinto ceremonies and accessories for the performances in the classic theatre are housed in the Homotsu-den treasury, where they can also be viewed. *Shrine complex: Daily 6.30am–5.30pm | Admission outside area free, inside area 500 ¥ | Treasury daily 9am–4pm | Admission 400 ¥, garden 500 ¥ | South-east of Nara Park*

KOFUKU TEMPLE

This main temple of the mighty Fujiwara clan was built in 710, and in its heyday consisted of 150 buildings. As with many wooden buildings, little of the originals remain following the ravages of fire and war. In fact, there are only a dozen left today, including the five-storey pagoda, the landmark of Nara. The temple houses the national treasury Kokuhokan – a museum with works of art that have been saved from all over the country. The east hall Tokondo dates back to the 15th century, and houses a famous statue of the 7th century. The temple is currently undergoing reconstruction, due for completion in 2018. *Temple site open all year round | Admission free | Treasury daily 9am–5pm | Admission 600 ¥ | Noborioji*

NARA PARK

The numerous temples and museums of the large park in the city centre contain almost all of the sights of the ancient imperial metropolis. It is also home to the 1200 holy deer, which can be extremely tame. You can buy special cookies for 150 ¥ to feed them.

NATIONAL MUSEUM

Built in 1895 and greatly extended in 1972, the museum contains treasures from the 6th to 8th centuries. The modern wing is dedicated to Buddhist art. Changing exhibitions are held in the old part. Imperial treasures from the Shoso-in are on display from around 20 October until the first week of November. *Tue–Sun 9.30am–5pm | Admission 520 ¥/, special exhibitions 830 ¥ | Nara Park*

TODAI-JI ⭐

The vast temple complex was founded in 745 by Emperor Shomu as the main site for all Buddhist temples in Japan. It is the main attraction in Nara. To get to the main hall, you walk through the Nandaimon gate of the 12th century, which is borne by 16 pillars. You will pass two particularly ferocious-looking "devas", Buddha's guards. These wooden figures by the sculptors Unkai and Kaikei of the Kamakura were created in the 13th century, have been extensively restored, and are some of the most artistically valuable sculptures in Japan. The Hall of the Great Buddha is well worth a visit. Although it has shrunk to two-thirds of its former size following various reconstructions, at 57 m/187 ft long, 50.5 m/165.7 ft wide and 48.7 m/159.8 ft high, it is still considered the tallest wooden building in the world. Inside, on a bronze pedestal in the shape of a lotus flower, is the Great Buddha *(Daibutsu)* made of bronze. His right hand means peace, the left fulfilment of wishes. 437 t of bronze, 130 kg of gold and 7 t of wax were used to cast the statue, which stands over 16 m/52.5 ft high. The original of 749 is said to have been one-third higher. Historians explain the excessive use of materials, thought to have been wasteful even then, as an attempt by Emperor Shomu to halt a devastating smallpox epidemic that not only cost the lives of countless people, but also undermined the Tenno's power.

Even though size and weight are no guarantee of beauty, the sheer scale of the statue is impressive. But much of what is said about the statue is nonsense, for instance that it is possible to climb through the nostrils of the almost 5-m/16.4-ft head with an open umbrella. A cute story: look on the back of the Buddha for a wooden pillar with a small opening. It is said that if you force yourself through the opening, you will find enlightenment. Children can do it – backwards, feet first – with ease, and thoroughly enjoy doing so. *Nov–Feb 8am–4.30pm, March 8am–5pm, April–Sep 7.30am–5.30pm, Oct 7.30am–5pm | Admission 500 ¥ | Nara Park*

Shoso-in: A short walk to the north of the Daibutsu will bring you to the old imperial treasury. The humidity inside the wooden building is automatically adjusted by the climate causing the beams to expand and contract. However, the treasures have been housed in the National Museum of Nara since 1963. The building can only be seen from the outside.

Kaidan-in: West of the Daibutsu, this hall houses famous clay figures of the Four Kings of Heaven. This used to be where priests were ordained. *Opening hours as for Todai-ji | Admission 400 ¥*

Nigatsu-do: A few stone steps lead from the Hall of the Great Buddha to this hall in the east, where the Omizutory festival – the sacred water-drawing festival – is held every year from 1 to 14 March after midnight, a special ordination period for the monks of this temple. From here, there is a picturesque ☀ city panorama at dusk. *Opening hours as for Todai-ji | Admission free*

Sangatsu-do: This is the oldest building in the complex, and houses a fine collection of figures from the Nara period (710–794). *Opening hours as for Todai-ji | Admission 500 ¥*

FOOD & DRINK

HIYORI

Traditional and extremely popular vegetarian restaurant where tofu, sea cucumbers and algae play the main roles. The menu also features regional dishes. *Wed–Mon lunchtime and evening | tel. 0742 24 14 70 | www.narakko.com/hiyori | Moderate*

INSIDER TIP STEAK CIEL BLEU

Its speciality is *teppanyaki*, fillet steak prepared on a hotplate with lobster and mussels in front of the guest. *Daily lunchtime and evenings | tel. 080 97 58 26 58 | steak-cielbleu.com | Expensive*

YOSHIKAWA TEI

The best deal in this French bistro is the three-course set lunch. *Tues–Sun | 1st Floor San-Fukumura Building | tel. 0742 23 76 75 | Moderate*

WHERE TO STAY

HOTEL FUJITA NARA

Very good mid-class hotel in a central location, convenient for reaching many of the sights. *117 rooms | Shimosanjo | tel. 0742 23 81 11 | www.fujita-nara.com | Budget*

NARA HOTEL

One of the few hotels in Japan that could be considered a grand hotel: high ceilings in the old building. A little old fashioned, but that's the Japanese idea of European tradition. The Japanese breakfast is considered a delicacy. *132 rooms | Takabatake | tel. 0742 26 33 00 | www.narahotel.co.jp | Moderate*

WASHINGTON HOTEL PLAZA NARA

Reliable business hotel in the best tourist location. The restaurant offers excellent, reasonable Japanese cuisine. *204 rooms | Shimosanjocho | tel. 0742 27 04 10 | washington.jp/nara/en | Budget*

INFORMATION

NARA CITY TOURIST CENTER

Excellent city map "Strolling around Nara". Will also find a voluntary tour guide. You pay any costs that incur on the tour. *Daily 9am–9pm | Nara-shi | tel. 0742 27 22 23*

WHERE TO GO

HORYU-JI (153 F3) (*∅ E8*)

Many myths and legends surround the oldest preserved temple in Japan (606). This is where Prince Regent Shotoku once lived, who is considered the patron of Japanese Buddhism. According to the legend, he was already able to meditate standing up shortly after he was born. A statue in the treasury testifies to this. The significance of the vast complex with 45 listed buildings – including 17 that are classed as valuable cultural treasures – is that it contains what are probably the oldest wooden buildings in the world arranged in one of the loveliest temple complexes in East Asia. The complex consists of the West Temple *(Sai-in)* and the East Temple *(To-in)*. In the western part, the five-storey pagoda of 607 and the Golden Hall *(Kondo)* create an asymmetrical counterpart to the rear reading hall *(Daikodo)*. Four recesses on the ground floor of the pagoda contain Buddhist scenes: two Bodhisattva in the east, Buddha's entry to Nirvana in the north, the burning of Buddha's bones in the west, and the paradise of the future Buddha in the south. The Buddha Shakyamuni triad in the main hall *(Kondo)* is one of the biggest Buddhist treasures in Japan. Unfortunately, the light is very poor. **INSIDER TIP** A torch will help. Go through the East Gate to get to the Hall of Dreams *(Yume-dono)*, the oldest octagonal wooden building in Japan. This is where the Prince Regent is said to have withdrawn for special meditations. Inside is the long-lost *Guze Kannon*, a 180 cm/5 ft 11 in tall statue that experts say is the loveliest in Japan. In 1993, the temple complex was the first Japanese site to be recognised by Unesco as a World Heritage Site. *Daily 8am– 4.30pm | Admission 1500 ¥ | 12 km/7.5 mi south-west of the city on JR station Horyu-ji-mae | www.horyuji.or.jp*

TOSHODAI-JI (153 F3) (*ω E8*)

In 759, Emperor Shomu had the priest and master builder Ganjin brought to Japan from the Middle Kingdom to *Nishi-no-Kyo (15min by bus from Nara)* for the construction of this temple, which is now the main seat of the Buddhist Ritsu sect. The statues that were set up there also came from China. The three fabulous Buddhas in the main hall *(Kondo)* in particular are well worth seeing, although a lacquered figure by Master Ganjin is only brought out on his birthday. Incidentally, it took six attempts for the Chinese priest to get here: on five occasions, he was prevented from making the journey by storms, a shipwreck and an abundance of bureaucracy. By the time he was finally able to start building, he had gone blind. Following a ten-year refurbishment, it is now possible to see the main hall *(Kondo)* again. *Daily 8.30am– 4.30pm | Admission 600 ¥ | Buses 52, 63, 70, 97, 98 from JR or Kintetsu station Nara to Yakushi-ji-higashiguchi*

Myth-enshrouded Horyu-ji: temple founder Shotoku was said to have meditated as a baby

OKAYAMA

(153 E3) (*D8*) 715,000 people live in the modern prefecture capital to the west of Honshu.

Okayama is an industrial city; rubber is one item that is produced here.

However, there are also a number of tourist attractions that make a visit worthwhile, such as the spectacular Seto Ohashi Bridge that spans the 9 km/5.6 mi to Shikoku Island. And of course the Koraku-en, one of the three loveliest gardens in Japan.

SIGHTSEEING

KORAKU-EN

The garden, which was completed in 1700, was the first garden in Japan to have vast lawns that are crowned by fabulously arranged bamboos, pine and cherry trees. *Daily April–Sep 7.30am–6pm, Oct–March 8am–5pm | Admission 400 ¥, with castle 560 ¥ | Naka | www.okayama-korakuen.jp*

OKAYAMA CASTLE ☆

The castle, which is visible from a great distance, was completed in the 16th century, and is one of the biggest fortresses in Japan. The black castle, from which you have a lovely view of the Koraku Garden, is commonly called "Crow Castle". The building was destroyed after the Meiji restoration and in WWII, and rebuilt in 1966. *Daily 9am–5pm | Admission 300 ¥ | Naka*

WHERE TO STAY

BENESSE HOTEL

Art in the hotel is the concept behind this establishment on Naoshima Island, which you get to by bus from Okayama to Uno, and then by ferry (hourly). The hotel was built by the architect Tadao Ando, and delights with its contemporary art. Next door is the Chichu Museum, which was also designed by Ando. *16 rooms | Naoshima, Kagawan-gun | tel. 087 8 92 20 30 | www.benesse-artsite.jp/en | Expensive*

INFORMATION

OKAYAMA CITY SIGHT SEEING OFFICE
JR Okayama station | tel. 086 2 22 29 12

OSAKA

🔲 **MAP ON PAGE 160**
(153 F3) (*E8*) Osaka is the eternal "second city". Economically, the city is overshadowed by the capital Tokyo, and culturally it is trumped by the old imperial residence Kyoto.

Japan's third-biggest city isn't necessarily an architectural beauty, but Osaka is unconventional, cheeky, hip, and always louder than the competition. Its citizens are said to be open, trendy and entertaining. And indeed, Osaka is the capital of Japan's comedians and gourmets, because the people also like to eat, eat

> 🏙 **WHERE TO START?**
> **Shinkansen station Shin-Osaka.** The station in the northern borough of Kita/Umeda, a business and administrative centre, is a good place to start a visit to Osaka. From here, the underground runs frequently to the districts Shinsaibashi and Namba, famous for their nightlife, for the shopping arcades for young and independent cultural trends.

well and eat a lot. The harbour city was Japan's first trade centre, and is still the busiest city in the oriental island empire. As the home of traditional industries, the region long suffered under the economic crisis. However, there is a mood of change among its 2.6 million inhabit-

on the roof. The 59-ac north side of the main station, which is used by 2.5 million people every day, has been modernised and is now a residential and entertainment area. The city fathers are also redesigning the river bank and bridges to the south, around the popular *Dotonbo-*

Kitschy and colourful, glittering and neon bright: Osaka's trendy quarter Dotonbori

ants. Osaka wants to be the "robot capital of the world".

Administration and private industry are organising the research and development of the relevant technology together. In order to revitalise the industry, a number of "bio-clusters", biotechnical research centres, are also being supported. The city is reinventing itself as well. In the administrative and business region Umeda in the north, shopping and entertainment centres such as the *Herbis Ent* with restaurants and boutiques as well as a theatre and concert hall are being built. To the north are Japan's biggest underground mall and the ● shopping centre *Hep Five* , which has a Ferris wheel

ri pedestrian promenade. And by doing so, Osaka wants to have the attractive promenades that will finally allow it to live up to its image of the "World city of water" with 808 bridges. For the first time, promenades with smart cafés and ferry stations are being built. Not even Tokyo or Kyoto can keep up.

SIGHTSEEING

DEN-DEN TOWN

Originally the shopping area for electronics in Nipponbashi, this town – like Akihabara in Tokyo – has become a hotspot for subculture, especially for *Otaku*, the Japanese version of particularly

Umeda Sky Building:
twin towers with views

ments. It's a busy combination of kara-oke bars, Pachinko arcades and other places of entertainment. Warning: Do not allow yourself to be lured into a clip joint! The large crab outside *Kani-Dora-ku* restaurant is the symbol of the area you can safely walk around after dark – and in fact, should. Incidentally, you can also see this glittering world from afar, from Ebiso Bridge. It is a popular meeting place for the youth of Osaka and the countless Chinese tourists.

OPEN-AIR MUSEUM

Eleven traditional farmhouses were brought here from all over the country, and rebuilt exactly like the originals in the Hattori Ryokuchi Park in the north of Osaka. Each one represents a particular region's typical building style. *Tue–Sun 9.30am–5pm | Admission 500 ¥ | Ryoku-chi-koen | www.occh.or.jp/minka*

MUSEUM OF ORIENTAL CERAMICS

One of the loveliest collections of Chinese and Korean ceramics with over 1300 items in the northern suburb of Kita-ku. The display includes two national treasures and 13 other works of art that are rated as significant. *Tue–Sun 9.30am–5pm, admission until 4.30m, closed on public holidays | Admission 500 ¥ | Kita | www.moco.or.jp*

OSAKA CASTLE

One of the most magnificent and historically most important castles in Japan dominates the skyline of Osaka. This impressive reconstruction on the original foundations in the great park of the city houses a number of excellent exhibitions on the history of the impressive building, as well as on the pre-eminent daimyo and warrior Toyotomi Hideyoshi who had the supposedly impregnable fortress built in 1583 during the feudal war for the

intense fans or nerds. In addition to shops for computers and accessories, there is also a wealth of Maid cafés and shops with Cosplay, anime and manga.

DOTONBORI ★

The lively quarter on the eponymous river is Osaka's popular promenading and nightlife area with pedestrian zones, theatres, gaudy neon advertising and kitschy-colourful restaurant advertise-

unification of Japan as a sign of his power. It is said that around 100,000 labourers worked on its construction. Thirty-two years after Hideyoshi's death, his opponent Tokugawa Ieyasu had the fortress destroyed and rebuilt, but over the course of time it was repeatedly destroyed or burnt down. Today's main tower was built in 1931. There are wonderful panoramic views of Osaka and the surrounding area from the ☀ observation platform on the seventh floor. *Daily 9am–5pm, closed 28 Dec–1 Jan | Admission 600 ¥ | Chuo | www.osakacastle.net*

PANASONIC CENTER ☺

The latest high-tech electronic products and developments are displayed in the exhibition centre of the electronics giant Panasonic. In order to resist pressure from the competition, the company is increasingly opting for environmentally friendly products and eco systems. *Daily 10am–8pm | Admission free | Umekita | tel. 06 63 77 17 00 | panasonic.net/center/osaka*

SPA WORLD ●

The biggest spa complex in the world in the south of the city comprises 16 different spas from eleven countries, including a Hammam (Turkish steam bath), a Japanese onsen and a bathing landscape. These culture baths are segregated by gender. On the roof is an "aquaresort" with pools, slides and restaurants for young and old. *Daily 10am–8.45pm | Admission day ticket Mon–Fri 2700 ¥, Sat/Sun 3000 ¥, 3 hrs 2400 ¥ or 2700 ¥ | Naniwa | tel. 06 66 31 00 01 | www.spaworld.co.jp/english*

SUMIYOSHITAISHA SHRINE ●

The main temple of all Sumiyoshi shrines in the eponymous borough is said to protect the well-being of families and travellers. It was built in the 3rd century to the Shinto deities of the seas to commemorate the safe passage of an empress to Korea. The complex, which still contains a number of precise reconstructions of the 3rd century, is rare in that it was created before Japan's Shinto architecture was influenced by Chinese Buddhism. Thus, for instance, the roofs of the main buildings are thatched rather than tiled. *Daily 6am–5pm | Admission free | Sumiyoshi | www.sumiyoshitaisha.net*

INSIDER TIP ▶ TEMPOZAN ☀

The travel time to Tempozan is 20 minutes on the Chuo metro. It's well worth making the trip to the coast because the flair of the harbour town Osaka is especially lively here. The main attraction is what is at 112 m/367 ft the second largest Ferris wheel *(daily 10am–10pm | 800 ¥)* in the world (after the London Eye). The views of Osaka, the bay and neighbouring Kobe are simply unbeatable, especially in the evening, with the sparkling lights of the two cities. Also well worth a visit are the *Tempozan Harbor Village* shopping centre with its numerous shops and restaurants *(daily 11am–8pm)* and the *Aquarium Kaiyukan* (see p. 131), one of the biggest in the world.

UMEDA SKY BUILDING ☀

An architectural eye-catcher with fabulous views near the station in the northern centre Umeda, this 170-m/558-ft skyscraper was built in 1994. It consists of two twin towers made of glass that are connected by a bridge on the 37th floor. You have fabulous all-round views of the city and harbour from the observation platform *Floating Garden Observatory,* which is reached via a spectacular escalator. *Daily 10am–10pm | Admission 700 ¥ | Kita*

Film fun at Universal Studios

INSIDER TIP **UNIVERSAL STUDIOS**

Cinema-lovers play the main part in the Hollywood theme park. In "Jurassic Park", all that will save you from a rampaging dinosaur is a breathtaking leap into a 29-m/95.1-ft abyss and complete darkness. "Back to the Future" catapults you from the future into the past. And in "E.T.", the extra-terrestrial and his visitor ride a bicycle around the room. Expect long queues at the various attractions. *Daily 9am–9pm | Single-day ticket 7200 ¥, 2 days 12,100 ¥ | Universal City | tel. 06 64 65 30 00 | www.usj.co.jp*

FOOD & DRINK

There are lots of good restaurants in the Dotonburi-dori shopping precinct in Namba, Minami.

DAIKOKU

Well-known tofu and fish restaurant. The house speciality is *kayaku-gohan*, a dish consisting of rice, tofu and various vegetables – reasonable and nutritious. *Closed Sun | Dotonbori | tel. 06 62 111101 | Budget*

KANI-DORAKU

This restaurant in Dotonbori with the giant crab outside serves crabs that the Japanese love so much. Famous establishment with long waiting times. Better to get on the daily bookings list in plenty of time. *Daily 11am–11pm | tel. 06 62 11 89 75 | Budget–Moderate*

MATSUYA GYU YAKINIKU M

Serves Matsuya beef, one of the three major Japanese Wagyu varieties, grilled or fried, at reasonable prices. *Daily noon–3pm and 5pm–midnight | Namba | tel. 06 62 11 29 04 | Moderate*

MIMIU HONTEN

This upmarket restaurant in Chuo creates the Osakan noodle speciality *udon suki* from chicken, shrimps, clams and seasonal vegetables. It is freshly prepared at your table. *Mon–Sat 11.30am–9.30pm | tel. 06 62 315770 | Moderate*

MIZUNO

Popular establishment serving the speciality *okonomiyaki*. Locals swear by this Japanese version of pizza that is healthy, nutritious, inexpensive and doesn't take long to prepare. *Daily 11am–11pm | Dotonbori | tel. 06 62 12 63 60 | Budget*

ENTERTAINMENT

INSIDER TIP **NATIONAL BUNRAKU THEATRE**

The colourful performances at this traditional puppet theatre, plays and love stories can go on for hours. To see what you think, watch an act or two (each about 30 min) first. Each puppet – they are about half the size of a normal adult – is operated by three people. The story on the stage is narrated by story-tellers in a dramatic sing-song and accompanied by shamisen music. English explanations are a new addition. The admission price varies, depending on the performance. *Chuo | tel. 06 62 12 25 31*

SKY LOUNGE STARDUST

The views of the glittering cities of Osaka and Kobe from the 39th floor of the Umeda Sky Building are breathtaking. The bar offers 100 cocktails, 50 different whiskies, 50 wines and selected liqueurs. *Mon–Fri 5pm–11.30pm, Sat/Sun 5pm–11pm | tel. 06 64 40 38 90*

WHERE TO STAY

HILTON OSAKA

Modern establishment at the Osaka JR station with 525 rooms and excellent restaurants (including western cuisine). Pool and gym. Central location, surrounded by a large shopping centre. *Kita | tel. 06 63 47 71 11 | www.hilton.com | Moderate*

NEW OTANI

540 rooms, many of them with wonderful views of the castle, excellent sports facilities with indoor and outdoor pools as well as 15 restaurants. *Chuo | tel. 06 69 41 11 11 | newotani.co.jp/osaka | Expensive*

OSAKA NAMBA GUEST HOUSE

Very reasonable private accommodation in Namba (7 min to Namba station). The owner is very friendly and extremely helpful. *3 rooms, 1 bathroom | tel. 09 39 75 02 25 | www.hostelbookers.com/hostels/japan/Osaka | Budget*

OSAKA TOKYU REI HOTEL

Very good mid-class hotel in the heart of the city. *402 rooms | Kita | tel. 06 63 15 01 09 | www.tokyuhotelsjapan.com/en | Moderate*

SUNROUTE UMEDA

Reasonable 3-star business hotel near Hankyu Umeda station with small but clean rooms. *217 rooms | tel. 06 63 73 11 11 | Budget*

INFORMATION

VISITORS INFORMATION CENTRE

Osaka station, main hall north side | tel. 06 63 45 21 89 | www.osaka–info.jp/en

WHERE TO GO

KOYA-SAN (153 F3) (*∅ E8*)

Those seeking peace and self-knowledge in Japan will find them in the lodgings offered by the Shukubo monks on the temple mountain Koya-san, 90 minutes by train from Osaka. At an altitude of 900 m/2953 ft are 58 monasteries that offer overnight accommodation in the temples in rooms that are quite sparsely furnished, often containing nothing more than a futon mat, but providing delicious, usually vegetarian evening meals and a Japanese breakfast. In Japan, Koya-san is also called the "Mountain of Hermits", regardless of which, though, more than a million pilgrims come here every year to pray. Foreigners enjoy *Rengejo-in (tel. 0736 5 60 06 | reservations also through Tourist Association Koyosan Kanko Kyokai: tel. 0736 56 26 16 | Budget*) with 48 guestrooms and famous for its tofu and the altar room for meditation (also in English).

SOUTHERN JAPAN

"Un bel dì, vedremo" – who isn't familiar with the emotional aria of longing sung by Madama Butterfly in Puccini's opera? It is so easy to imagine her looking out over Nagasaki's natural harbour, constantly waiting for her lover to return from a foreign country. The beauty in the kimono and her gentleman from the west, plus the soft pink cherry blossom – there has probably never been a stronger cliché of Japan.

In Nagasaki in the Middle Ages, Nippon opened up from its feudal isolation. The first European traders landed here, and the Christianisation of Japan began. Thanks to its cheerful atmosphere, Nagasaki is still the point of attraction of Japan's third largest island Kyushu, which has a total population of 14.5 million.

BEPPU

(152 C4) (*M C9*) **Steam rises on the edge of the road, the smell of sulphur is in the air: Beppu (pop. 125,000) is the El Dorado of thermal spas (onsen) in Japan.**

You will find the best spas near the station, and the most popular one is *Takegawara (daily 6.30am–10.30pm | admission 60, sand bath plus 600 ¥)* with a lovely sand bath. *Kannawa Onsen (daily 6.30am–8pm | admission 510 ¥)* in the *Shibaseki Onsen (daily 7am–8pm | admission 210 ¥, family bath 1620 ¥ hr)* includes a communal pool without gender segregation, which has become rare. You can also hire a *kazokuburo,* a family bath.

Visit hell in Beppu and dream with Madama Butterfly in Nagasaki – you really shouldn't miss Japan's south

SIGHTSEEING

THE "HELLS" OF KANNAWA ★

Locals call the springs the "Hells" because of the extreme temperatures, and use the water for heating or cooking. More than 1 million hectolitres are pumped every day. The springs are all slightly different. *Umi-jigoku*, "Sea Hell", is an intense blue water of 98 degrees Celsius that contains sulphur and iron. This spring was discovered 1200 years ago. *Chi-no-ike-jigoku*, "Blood Pond Hell", is deep red with massive clouds of steam rising up out of the little lake. Mud sloshes around in *Kamado-jigoku*, "Boiling Hell". *Yama-jigoku,* "Demon Mountain Hell", is like a rock that is constantly swathed in mist and steam. And *Tatsumaki-jigoku* "Geyser Hell", is, as you would imagine, a geyser. It spews hot water into the sky every 30 minutes. You can then admire the eruption for three minutes.

Six of the nine most famous hot springs of Beppu are within walking distance of each other, while the others are about

Hot spring for tremendous healing: there's much steaming, bubbling and spouting in Beppu

1 km/0.6 mi outside Kannawa. But the INSIDER TIP *Jigoku Meguri Circuit Pass* allows you to visit all the "Hells". *Daily 8am–5pm | Admission 2100 ¥, individually 500 ¥*

WHERE TO STAY

SAKARYA MINSHUKU
The oldest guesthouse in town with all the charm of the Meiji period (1868–1912). The stone oven in the courtyard is fed by a hot spring. *12 rooms | Ida, Kannawa | tel. 0977 66 62 34 | Budget*

INFORMATION

BEPPU CITY TOURIST INFORMATION
Kaminoguchi | tel. 0977 211128 | www.city.beppu.oita.jp

FUKUOKA

(152 B4) (*ш B8*) **Strictly speaking, the 1.5 million people in this, the biggest metropolis north of Kyushu, live in two different cities.**

To the west is Fukuoka, generally more middle-class, while to the east is proletarian Hakata. The two were merged in 1889, but each guards its ownership status closely. Shinkansen terminus, for instance, is called Hakata, but the airport was named after Fukuoka.

The city has a cosmopolitan flair. It's a great place for shopping and partying. And it's the only place in Japan where you'll find a beach promenade in the middle of the city. Fukuoka is also considered the "Cradle of Japanese Civilisation". Historic finds indicate that people had already settled here in 300 BC.

SIGHTSEEING

CANAL CITY
Consumer and party paradise with an interesting architecture, numerous boutiques and bistros, and 13 cinemas. There is an amphitheatre beside a man-made river. *Hakata | www.canalcity.co.jp*

FUKUOKA MUSEUM OF ART

One of the best collections of contemporary Asian art and a library. *Tue–Sun 9.30am–5pm | Admission 200 ¥ | 7th/8th floor of the Hakata Riverain Complex | Kawabata*

FUKUOKA CITY MUSEUM

On display are examples of the cultural connections between Japan and its Asian neighbours, which include a very old gold seal that bears witness to the historic associations between Japan and China. *Tue–Sun 9.30am–5.30pm | Admission 200 ¥ | Momochi*

FUKUOKA TOWER ⚡

City landmark, and at 234 m/768 ft the most eye-catching building. There are lovely views from *Café Dart* at dusk. There is a viewing platform deck at 234 m/768 ft. *Daily April–Sep 9.30am–9pm, Oct–March 9.30am–10pm | Admission 800 ¥, 20% discount with a foreign passport | www.fukuokatower.co.jp/english*

FOOD & DRINK

INSIDER TIP MAGURO NO YAKATA
Very reasonable sushi on a conveyor belt is available in Downtown (near Daimaru department store). *Daily Watanabe-dori | tel. 0927316030 | Budget*

INSIDER TIP NAGAHAMA RAMEN
Fukuoka is famous for its ramen noodle soups. There's an unbeatable choice in this district near the docks: shop after shop, usually open-air – with plenty for all tastes (including vegetarian). The nearest underground station is Akasaka. *www.kyushu.com/fukuoka/restaurants/nagahama_ramen | Budget*

WHERE TO STAY

HILTON FUKUOKA SEA HAWK
The large complex is located right on the beach promenade, near a shopping and entertainment quarter. Some rooms are furnished in the Japanese style. *1052 rooms | Chuo | tel. 0928 44 8111 | www.hiltonfukuokaseahawk.jp | Moderate*

HOTEL NIKKO FUKUOKA
The best hotel with 359 rooms. *Hakata | tel. 092 4821111 | www.hotelnikko-fukuoka.com | Moderate*

INFORMATION

FUKUOKA CITY TOURIST INFORMATION
JR station Hakata | tel. 0924313003

★ **The "Hells" of Kannawa**
Boiling hot springs: There's a constant steaming, bubbling and spouting in the famous spas of Beppu → p. 101

★ **Sakurajima**
The active volcano at Kagoshima spits out ash on an almost daily basis → p. 104

★ **Glover Garden**
Pure romance: Even from a distance, you'll hear Madama Butterfly in the park in Nagasaki → p. 106

★ **Battlefield**
Japan at the end of WWII: hundreds of thousands of soldiers died near Okinawa → p. 111

MARCO POLO HIGHLIGHTS

WHERE TO GO

KUMAMOTO (152 B5) (*🕮 B9*)

This is the most German town in Japan. This university town (pop. 735,000) 70 km/43.5 mi from Nagasaki has German bakers and butchers, restaurants and pubs, a German choir and a group for German games. A significant proportion of the people here have been involved with Germany in some way, either as exchange students, university students, as guest families or as tourists. Why: Heidelberg is the partner town of Kumamoto.

The castle ruins are well worth a visit *(daily 8.30am–6pm, 5pm in winter | admission 500 ¥ | Honmaru)*. The fortress, which is almost 400 years old, is one of the three most famous in Japan. In 1877, the last of the Samurai gathered here in an uprising against the empire. Their defeat – the subject of the film "The Last Samurai" with Tom Cruise – sealed the end of the feudal age in Japan.

It's a short walk from the castle to the *Hotel Nikko Kumamoto (191 rooms | Kamitori | tel. 0962111111 | www.nikko-kumamoto.co.jp | Moderate)*, which has rooms to European standards.

KAGOSHIMA

(152 B6) (*🕮 A10*) **Those Japanese who like making comparisons call the southernmost metropolis of Kyushu the "Naples of the East" – a slightly poisoned chalice.**

This city is only attractive when Sakurajima, its version of Vesuvius, is not active – which is only very rarely the case. Its population of just over 605,000 will often open umbrellas as protection against the heavy dust downpours that waft over from the other side of Kinko Bay. Sometimes the streets and cars are centimetres thick in dust.

Saint Francis Xavier commenced his catholic missionary work in 1549. For 29 generations and almost eight centuries, the Shimazu clan ruled from here – far from the capital – over the fortunes of the land from Southern Japan to Okinawa.

SIGHTSEEING

ISO-TEIEN (SENGANEN)

The Shimazu clan was responsible for the city's loveliest attraction: the castle park with plum trees and bamboo groves, picturesquely located in a bay that also has the royal residence. Fabulous poetry festivals were held by a small river in aristocratic times, at which every participant had to quickly write a poem before the next sake barrel floated down the river. Unfortunately, the park is not as well tended as the tourist brochures claim. *Daily 8.30am–5.30pm | Admission 1000 ¥ | North of the city centre*

SAKURAJIMA ★

In 1914, the volcano spouted 3 million tons of lava into the strait, burying several villages, and leaving a 400 m/1312 ft wide and 70 m/229.7 ft deep link between the island and the mainland. The last eruption was in 1960. Since 1955, one of the three cones has constantly being spewing out smoke, and often ash as well. Some parts of the island look like a moon landscape, while others are extremely fertile. Radishes weighing up to 35 kg and with a diameter of up to 1½ m/4.9 ft grow here. Climbing the volcano is not allowed, but there are a number of good lookout points all around. There are ferries every 15 minutes from a pier near the station.

FOOD & DRINK

KUMASTOEI
No. 1 address for regional delicacies. The extensive menu (which is also in English) contains fish, vegetable, chicken

airport. *247 rooms | Yojiro | tel. 099 2 53 20 20 | www.sunroyal.co.jp | Budget*

KAGOSHIMA TOKYU HOTEL ☙
Hotel beside the water, balcony with volcano views. *206 rooms | Kamoike |*

View of the fire mountain: there is always a cloud of smoke over the volcano Sakurajima

and pork specialities in countless variations. Booking is recommended. *Daily 11am–2pm and 5pm–9.30pm | tel. 099 2 22 63 56 | Moderate*

SHOCHU TENGOKU
150 different varieties of *shochu* – more types of the rice and sweet potato spirit than anywhere else – certainly justify the name of the "Schnaps paradise" bar. *Mon–Sat 5pm–midnight | Edo Yoshi Building | Yamanokuchi | tel. 099 2 24 97 50 | Budget*

WHERE TO STAY

KAGOSHIMA SUN ROYAL HOTEL
Situated on the promenade, good traffic links. There is also a shuttle to the

tel. 099 2 57 24 11 | www.tokyuhotels japan.com/en | Moderate

INFORMATION

TOURIST INFORMATION CENTER
JR station Nishi-Kagoshima | tel. 099 2 53 25 00

WHERE TO GO

INSIDER TIP ▶ **CHIRAN** (152 B6) *(ὑ B10)*
This small town (pop. 14,000, 37 km/ 23 mi from Kagoshima) is well worth a visit for its Samurai alley consisting of seven old residences with glorious gardens. No. 7 of 1741 is particularly well preserved. The carefully planned winding road reveals the tactics behind the

feudal warriors' defence system. At the side is a stream with large, colourful ornamental carp.

YAKUSHIMA (155 D2) (*Ⓜ B10*)

The granite island of the Nansai Group is a Unesco World Heritage Site. The most famous Japanese cedars grow on the rocks that rise up to 1935 m/6348 ft above sea level, and are said to be the inspiration behind some of the scenes in Miyazaki Hayao's classic "Princess Mononoke".

The island, which is home to 14,000 people, is also a place of meteorological extremes. The peaks are snow-covered in winter, but you can also go for a swim on its beaches. The main attractions are walks and hikes through the moss green forests with 1900 plant species. Spend the night (half-board) at the *Seaside Hotel (80 rooms | tel. 0997 42 01 75 | www. ssh-yakushima.co.jp | Budget)*

NAGASAKI

(152 B5) (*Ⓜ B9*) **Warm summer nights in the picturesque bay, lanterns in the gardens, kimono-clad beauties: Nagasaki (pop. 44,000) is the main attraction on Kyushu for its cheerful, charming atmosphere.**

You can feel the European flair in many places, and gain an impression of what it was like when Nagasaki opened Japan's door to the rest of the world. Nowhere else are there so many churches: this is where Japan's christianisation by Portuguese missionaries began, but ended abruptly with the crucifixion slaughter of 1597. Seventeen years after the martyrdom of 26 European and Japanese, the country banned the western religion completely, persecuted and brutally murdered Christians, and expelled foreigners. Only the little island of Deji-

ma remains as a trade enclave. So even in the darkest days, western knowledge and culture still managed to reach the isolated empire. After the Meiji opening, the city with the natural harbour quickly became a centre for ship-building. On 9 August 1945, an American bomber dropped an atomic bomb on Nagasaki, destroying almost half the city.

The Shianbashi Centre, where locals go to shop and eat, is 2 km/1.2 mi from the JR station. From there, you can walk through China Town to the Holland Slopes and Glover Garden in the south.

SIGHTSEEING

DEJIMA

This tiny, man-made island was once the eye in Japan's needle to the rest of the world. Today it is difficult to explore, but a museum at the tram stop Dejima provides information. A handful of Dutch merchants lived on Dejima for about 200 years, completely isolated from Japanese life. The only people who had access to them apart from their trade partners were monks and prostitutes. *Daily 8am–6pm | Admission 510 ¥*

DUTCH SLOPE

After the opening of Japan, this cobbled path was flanked by the wooden homes built for foreigners. For the sake of simplicity, they were just all considered Dutch. Some of the houses have been rebuilt. One that is particularly impressive is Junibankan, built in 1868, and once the site of the Prussian Consulate in Nagasaki. *Shiminbyoin*

GLOVER GARDEN ★

From a distance, you can already hear the famous motif of Madama Butterfly – sung by the Japanese opera singer Miura Tamaki (1884–1946), commemorated here by a life-size bronze statue. Otherwise, the story is pure legend. Thomas Glover, who resided here on this green hill above the harbour entrance from around 1900 until his death in 1911 and the most famous foreigner

the Mitsubishi shipyard; 75,000 civilians were killed, the same number injured. An annual memorial service, the Peace Memorial Ceremony, is held in the Peace Park, once the site of the main prison. The most eye-catching symbol is

In a kimono under a parasol: traditionally-minded girls on the island of Dejima

in Nagasaki, was a Scot and not, as Giacomo Puccini's opera "Madama Butterfly" would have it, an American. The atmosphere of the first western villas in Japan can still be felt today. Built in 1863, the ✵ Glover Mansion, in the midst of a well-tended garden, offers wonderful views of the natural harbour. *Daily 8am–6pm, 8am–9.30pm in summer | Admission 610 ¥ | Minami-Yamate*

HYPOCENTER PARK

The park is north of the station, in the suburb of Urakami. A black stone commemorates the time and place (ground zero) of the atomic bomb explosion: 9 August 1945, 11.02am. The target was

the 10-m/32.8-ft Peace Statue. A visit to the Atomic Bomb Museum is a shattering experience. *Daily 8.30am–6.30pm, Sep–April 8.30am–5.30pm | Admission 200 ¥*

CONFUCIUS SHRINE SOFUKU-JI

The red entrance gate is a typical example of the architecture of the Chinese emperors during the Ming dynasty. The colourful pilgrimage site is the only Confucius mausoleum outside China. It contains 20 collected works, engraved in marble, reflecting the teachings of the great Chinese philosopher in 500 sections and 16,000 characters. It is said that during the dramatic famine

Confucius shrine: 72 of the philosopher's students, chiselled in marble

of 1653, up to 3000 needy were fed on gruel from the gigantic cooking pot on the temple grounds. *Daily 8am–5pm | Admission 300 ¥ | Kayiya*

OURA CHURCH

The church, which was built in 1864 for Catholic foreigners, is dedicated to the 26 Christians who were crucified in 1597. Despite the ban on religion for natives, Japanese believers also congregated here at the end of the 19th century. *Daily 8am–6pm | Admission 300 ¥ | Near Glover Park*

URAKAMI CHURCH

The cathedral, which was completed in 1914, was the biggest church in East Asia until its destruction by the atomic bomb. The new cathedral was built in 1959. *Daily 9am–5pm | Admission free | Moto*

FOOD & DRINK

HAMAKATSU

The menu contains Nagasaki specialities such as *shippoku,* a banquet-like meal for four people with Chinese, Portuguese and Japanese elements. *Daily 11.30am–8.30pm | Kajiya | tel. 095 8 26 83 21 | Moderate*

HARBIN

Gourmet establishment serving Russian-French cuisine. Reasonable lunchtime menus. *Daily 11.30am–2pm and 5.30–9pm | Yorosuja | tel. 095 8 24 66 50 | Moderate*

WHERE TO STAY

ANA CROWNE PLAZA

Popular and comfortable hotel at the foot of Glover Garden, with buffet restaurant. Ideal starting point for many of the sights. *216 rooms | tel. 095 8 18 66 01 | www.anacrowneplaza-nagasaki.jp | Budget*

HOTEL NEW NAGASAKI

Situated directly at the JR station, large gym and pool. *130 rooms | Daikoku | tel. 095 8 26 80 00 | www.newnaga.com | Moderate*

INFORMATION

NAGASAKI CITY TOURIST INFORMATION

JR station | tel. 095 8 23 36 31 | visit-nagasaki.com

OKINAWA

(154 B5–6) *(ﾉﾉ 0)* **When it comes to it, the Japanese on Okinawa (pop. 1.4 million) are also foreigners. Nippon's southernmost prefecture with the capital Naha is 2000 km/1243 mi from Tokyo, but only 200 km/124 mi from Taiwan's metropolis Taipei.**

In 1879, the main island of the Ryukyu archipelago became part of Japan, its language declared, without further ado, the "second main Japanese dialect". In 1945, the USA occupied the island for 27 years, and a number of US military bases remain there to this day. Although the locals demand that the Americans leave, they wouldn't dream of it: being so close to Taiwan is too important to them.

Apart from the region's typical "building sins", there is another architecture that catches the eye. A stone "spirit wall" screens the entrance to the houses, allegedly because bad spirits can only move in a straight line. Stone lion dogs called *shisa* guard the roofs and door posts. Okinawa has the INSIDER TIP highest number of centenarians in Japan – at the top of the league is the "Village of Eternal Youth", Ogimi. Scientists ascribe this to their exceptionally healthy diet and favourable social factors. The people on Okinawa are extremely active, they exercise outdoors, work in their gardens, go for lots of walks, and they love dancing the folk dances that follow the same movement sequences as tai chi. Around 80 percent of food served in Okinawa is plant based, and eaten raw, steamed or stir-fried in rapeseed oil. Life in Naha focuses around the 2-km/1.2-mi Boulevard Kokusai with hotels, bars, nightclubs and souvenir shops.

SIGHTSEEING

PEACE MEMORIAL MUSEUM

At the entrance to the former battlefield in Itoman (about 12 km/7.5 mi south of Naha), the Japanese view of the battle for Okinawa in WWII is presented. *Daily 9am–5pm | Admission 300 ¥*

SHURI CASTLE

As the headquarters of the imperial army, the former residence of the kings of Ryuku around 4 km/2.5 mi east of Naha was completely destroyed in the battle for Okinawa in 1945. The castle was rebuilt, exactly as it had been before, in 1993. *Daily 8.30am–6pm, 8.30am–8pm in summer | Admission 820 ¥ | Shuri*

FOOD & DRINK

Boiled pigs ears with ginger are the local speciality.

DOJO BAR

International pub for sports fans, especially lovers of karate and the martial sports. Tiny delicacies are served at the bar. *Daily 6pm–1am | tel. 098 9 11 36 01 | dojobarnara.com | Moderate*

LOW BUDGET

An authentic night's rest for little money: the *International Hostel Akari* in Nagasaki is a friendly establishment in the typical Japanese style. The hostel is in a central location, near the river and in the vicinity of the temples. A night's stay costs from 2500 ¥. *Kojiyai | tel. 095 8 01 79 00 | www.nagasaki-hostel.com*

TOYO HANTEN

Good Chinese food at reasonable prices in Chatan, about 16 km/9.9 mi from Naha. *Daily 11am–11pm | tel. 098 9 36 40 26 | Budget*

YUNANGI

Small and rustic, in Naha. House speciality: finely chopped pig's ear with cucumber and vinegar sauce. *Mon–Sat 11am–9pm | Kumochi | tel. 098 8 67 37 65 | Budget*

SHOPPING

Lovers of the exotic seek the libido enhancer habushu in Okinawa. Habus, the most dangerous venomous snakes in Okinawa, are seen in rearing positions, mouths wide open, in alcohol-filled jars or bottles – and they may be dead, but they're still pretty scary. The drink is said to work miracles when combined with black sugar or sweet potatoes. You will find original souvenirs such as these in little shops in the Heiwa-dori in the centre of Naha.

BEACHES

Okinawa's underwater world is one of the best diving regions in Eastern Asia. You'll find shimmering coral reefs with a colourful world of fish, impressive steep faces, bizarre caves and atmospheric grottos.

Moon Beach, Tiger Beach, Manza Beach and more: Okinawa's most popular beaches are in a line along the western coast, some 30 to 50 km/19 to 31 mi from Naha. There are smart hotels and lots of water sports offers all over.

WHERE TO STAY

INSIDER TIP ▶ BUSENA TERRACE RESORT
Japan's loveliest beach resort in Kise

with the most comfortable hotel in Okinawa combines Japanese perfection with Asian politeness and Mediterranean charm. The Busena also convinces with lovely open-air restaurants as well as artificial beaches. *401 rooms | tel. 098 511333 | www. terrace.co.jp | Expensive*

RITZ CARLTON NAGO

Exclusive, elegant and expensive: the first Ritz hotel on Okinawa in Nago with lovely beaches. Architecture and interior are adapted to the local area, as is the healthy and delicious cuisine in the *Teppanyaki* grill and the Okinawa restaurant *Gusuku*. The sports and wellness offerings – golf course, pool, spa and gym – are all spectacular. *79 rooms | tel. 0980 43 55 55 | www. ritzcarlton.com/en/Properties/Okinawa | Expensive*

Surrounded by a coral reef: picturesque beach on Sesoko, one of the 49 inhabited islands of Okinawa

INFORMATION

NAHA AIRPORT VISITOR INFORMATION CENTER
Airport | Kagamizu | tel. 098 8 57 68 84 | de.visitokinawa.jp

WHERE TO GO

GYOKUSEN-DO (154 B6) (*Ø 0*)
Japan's biggest limestone cave (35 km/ 21.8 mi south of Naha) was created 300,000 years ago and shows thousands of strange figures along a stretch of 1 km/0.6 mi. There is also a theme park and a historic reproduction of a village. *Daily 9am–6pm | Admission cave 1650 ¥ | www.gyokusendo.co.jp/okinawaworld/en*

BATTLEFIELD ★ (154 B6) (*Ø 0*)
The bloodiest battle against Japan ended in April 1945 with over 230,000 dead on the Japanese side alone. In the then naval headquarters – now the *Museum (daily 8.30am–5pm | admission 420 ¥)* – 4000 Japanese soldiers died by collective suicide. Civilians threw themselves to their deaths off *Cape Kyan*. At the southern tip *Himeyuri no To* teachers forced around 200 female students to jump off the cliffs to prevent them from falling into the hands of the Americans.

The memorial site focuses very much on the fates of the locals during the invasion and during the American occupation that followed. This single-mindedness also caused tremendous controversy among the international public. The government, prefectures and various associations have set up several monuments to make a park of national memorials on these historic sites. *12 km/7.5 mi south of Naha, with excursion buses departing from there*

DISCOVERY TOURS

① JAPAN AT A GLANCE

START: ❶ Tokyo station
END: ⓫ Nagasaki

13 days
Driving time
8 hours

Distance:
➡ 3272 km/2033 mi

COSTS: about 355,000 yen per person (Japan Rail Pass, taxis, accommodation, meals)
WHAT TO PACK: Small suitcases – in the Shinkansen, larger baggage items can only be placed in the last row of a carriage.

IMPORTANT TIPS: If you buy your Japan Rail Pass in Europe before you travel *(www.jrpass.com)*, you'll save a lot on the exchange rate! It is a good idea to book your hotels in advance.
Take taxis to the sights when you have any stops, as public transport requires local knowledge and an understanding of the language.

つなげよう、
日本。

Would you like to explore the places that are unique to this country? Then the Discovery Tours are just the thing for you – they include terrific tips for stops worth making, breathtaking places to visit, selected restaurants and fun activities. It's even easier with the Touring App: download the tour with map and route to your smartphone using the QR Code on pages 2/3 or from the website address in the footer below – and you'll never get lost again even when you're offline.

TOURING APP

→ p. 2/3

Travelling the country in what is said to be the most punctual train in the world, the Shinkansen, you will visit valuable temples and shrines, experience bustling harbour towns, stroll through traditionally landscaped gardens and bathe in hot springs.

Go to ❶ Tokyo station → p. 58 to board the Shinkansen. After 30 minutes you will arrive at ❷ Yokohama → p. 65. Stroll to the impressive **overseas harbour** and through lively **Chinatown**. In the evenings, enjoy the exotic cuisine in authentic restaurants and other eateries.

DAY 1
❶ Tokyo station 🚆
⎿ 31 km/19.3 mi ⏋
❷ Yokohama
🏙 🍽 🛏

Photo: Train driver on the high-speed Shinkansen

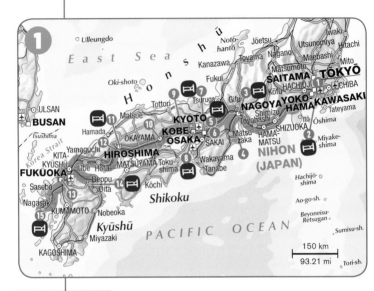

Continue your journey on the Shinkansen to **③ Nagoya → p. 49** (travel time approx. 1½ hours). After a visit to the impressive **castle → p. 49**, it's worth taking the express train to the **④ Ise-jingu → p. 50** and the original shrine of the Shinto (travel time 1½ hours).

Next morning, the Shinkansen will take you to **⑤ Kyoto → p. 74**, the classic Japan with 17 Unesco World Heritage Sites, in just half an hour. Allow four days in the old imperial metropolis to give yourself a chance to see the numerous temples and shrines, including a day trip (travel time 45 minutes) to the old imperial palace area **⑥ Nara → p. 88** with the fabulous temple site of **Todai-Ji → p. 91** and the Great Buddha. And the programme to contrast with it: **⑦ Osaka → p. 94** (travel time by Shinkansen 30 min), one of the most modern cities in the country. Stroll through the 'in' quarter of **Dotonbori → p. 96** with popular theatres, restaurants and bars. **Next day, continue to the busy harbour town** of **⑧ Kobe → p. 72**, which you can easily explore on foot. In the evening, enjoy the **cable car ride** up, the town's own mountain (400 m/ 1312 ft) **Rokko → p. 73** with fabulous views of the city and bay.

Next morning, there's a **40 min train ride** to **⑨ Himeji → p. 66**. You can see the famous castle **Himeji-jo**

DISCOVERY TOURS

→ **p. 66** from the station. It's a half-hour walk to this defence system, which is a popular backdrop for Samurai films. **Then a stop in** ⑩ **Okayama → p. 94** and a walk through **Koraku-en garden → p. 94**, which is a tram ride from the station. **After 45 min the Shinkansen stops in** ⑪ **Hiroshima → p. 69**. Allow three nights for this lively, modern harbour metropolis. Apart from a visit to the memorial sites of the 1945 atomic bomb, a boat ride to the romantic shrine island of ⑫ **Miyajima → p. 72** is a must. Its red water gate is the most frequently photographed landmark of Japan.

The Shinkansen takes you to ⑬ **Fukuoka/Hakata → p. 102** on the southern main island of **Kyu-shu** in 65 min. INSIDER TIP Stroll along the inner-city beach promenade before taking **a local train to the loveliest and wildest thermal baths in Japan in** ⑭ **Beppu → p. 100**. Be sure to take a dip in a hot spring, and spend a night in one of the many onsen hotels.

Back in Fukuoka/Hakata, **it's two hours on the express train to** ⑮ **Nagasaki → p. 106**, which is inextricably linked to Puccini's opera "Madama Butterfly".

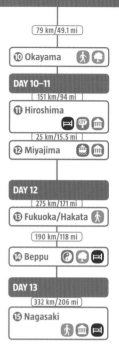

| 79 km/49.1 mi |
| ⑩ Okayama |

DAY 10–11
| 151 km/94 mi |
| ⑪ Hiroshima |
| 25 km/15.5 mi |
| ⑫ Miyajima |

DAY 12
| 275 km/171 mi |
| ⑬ Fukuoka/Hakata |
| 190 km/118 mi |
| ⑭ Beppu |

DAY 13
| 332 km/206 mi |
| ⑮ Nagasaki |

The train ride across the land offers frequent, delightful views of Mount Fuji

It's lovely to walk through romantic landscaped **Glover Garden** → **p. 106** and along the cobbled **Dutch Slope** → **p. 106**. The **Peace Park** → **p. 107** and **Urakami Church** → **p. 108** are memorials to the atomic bombing of 9 August 1945. We recommend choosing accommodation near the sights. Return to Tokyo via Fukuoka/Hakata on the Shinkansen.

② AT THE TOP OF MOUNT FUJI

START: ❶ Kawaguchiko	2 days
END: ❶ Kawaguchiko	Actual walking time
	9–11 hours

| Distance: easy | |
| 🚌 19 km/11.8 mi ▄▟ Height: 1476 m/4843 ft | |

COSTS: Approx. 955 yen admission as an environmental levy, accommodation in mountain huts approx. 4400 yen, hourly rate 955 yen per person
WHAT TO PACK: Strong hiking shoes or boots, rain jacket, sun screen warm clothing, torch, helmet recommended, water, snacks

IMPORTANT TIPS: It is only worth doing this tour in summer (July/August), when the huts are open and the buses go up to 2400 m/7874 ft. Those of average fitness with no mountain experience will manage the ascent, what is challenging is the increasingly thin air. Climbing Mount Fuji is a popular activity! So expect to encounter lots of other hikers.
Allow plenty of breaks, not least because of the differences in altitude and temperature (it's only about 5 degrees Celsius/41 degrees Fahrenheit at the top in summer!). There are no huts on the descent.

At 3776 m/12,388 ft, Mount Fuji is not only the highest and loveliest mountain in the country, but also a holy mountain for the Japanese. In order to experience the real Fuji feeling and be at the ★ peak of Fuji at sunrise, start walking the afternoon before and spend the night in a mountain hut.

The starting point is ❶ **Kawaguchiko** (express bus from Tokyo from Shinjuku station). **There, take the Fuji-Subaru line bus to** ❷ **Station 5** at about 2300 m/7546 ft. The six to eight hour ascent up the **Yoshida Trail** starts as a wide path, past crippled pines and grasses, then continues in a zigzag past volcanic and hard rock. You'll have the company of hundreds of other hikers from all over the world, wanting to climb Fuji.

All along the route you will pass small stands that sell six-edged walking sticks with gold-coloured bells – so you can get your very own "glockenspiel" to accompany you on your walk.

Once the route has wound its way up a further 400 m/ 1312 ft, you will arrive at ❸ **Station 7** where you can rest by the hour on futons in the common room *(telephone bookings only: tel. 05 55 23 65 23)* and enjoy a hot meal (curry and rice with beef). Or fortify yourself with hot and cold non-alcoholic drinks, soups, confectionery and instant noodles.

Continue towards the peak, and there you will reach a **kiosk** for refreshments at ❹ **Station 8** at 3100 m/ 10,171 ft. **The final and at the same time most difficult section awaits you 300 m/984 ft higher.** Before that, though, you can rest your weary body at the ❺ **Fujisan Hotel** *(350 beds, booking essential | tel. 05 55 22 19 47, summer only tel. 05 55 24 65 16 | Budget)*, a very basic establishment with a large mattress store. In clear weather, this is a good place to enjoy the fabulous panoramic views of the lights of Tokyo and Yokohama.

Expect a short night, though, because the students who run the "hotel" wake their guests up around 2am. On to the final stretch: **the last leg, which is pretty steep and rocky, will take you approximately 80 minutes** (possibly longer if there is a jam of visitors blocking the peak). Then comes the highlight of the whole tour: a fabulously colourful sunrise with panoramic views of the ❻ **peak. Once you have seen enough, walk the path around the inside of the crater (3.5 km/2.2 mi).** For centuries, people have walked this path in a clockwise direction. **After that, three hours of walking downhill on specially laid gravel paths back to Station 5, and finally take the bus back to** ❶ **Kawaguchiko.**

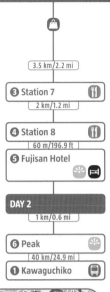

3.5 km/2.2 mi

❸ Station 7

2 km/1.2 mi

❹ Station 8

60 m/196.9 ft

❺ Fujisan Hotel

DAY 2

1 km/0.6 mi

❻ Peak

40 km/24.9 mi

❶ Kawaguchiko

RURAL SOUTH

3

START: ❶ Takamatsu
END: ❶ Takamatsu

3 days
Driving time
8 hours

Distance:
🚗 approx. 450 km/280 mi

COSTS: Japan Rail pass, meals, accommodation, taxis and admission fees approx. 85,000 yen per person
WHAT TO PACK: Rain jacket, sunscreen, swimming gear

IMPORTANT TIPS: Travel there by air, ferry, train or bus. Shikoku is very easy to explore by train. Maps are available from the tourist office next to the JR station, further tips for the island are available on the website *www.tourismshikoku.com*.

Discover the original Japan, far from the major cities, on Shikoku, the smallest of Japan's four main islands. Wander through traditional landscaped gardens, perspire in the bathhouse and watch whales and dolphins along the spectacular rugged coastline.

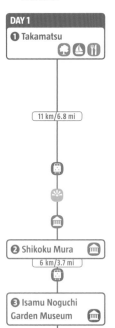

DAY 1

❶ Takamatsu

[11 km/6.8 mi]

❷ Shikoku Mura
[6 km/3.7 mi]

❸ Isamu Noguchi
Garden Museum

The starting point is the harbour town ❶ **Takamatsu** north of Shikoku. First comes **Ritsurin-koen**, one of the most famous historical gardens in Japan *(daily from sunrise to sunset | admission 410 ¥ | ritsuringarden.jp)* and a masterpiece of Japanese landscaping. Japan's biggest landscaped garden with its ponds, hills and bridges, rock formations, tea houses, cherry, plum and maple trees, is a delight for the eye all year round. Feel like a feudal lord on a leisurely **boat trip** *(30 min 610 ¥)*, then treat yourself to some sanuki udon, a thinner type of noodle **Ueharaya-honten** *(daily 10am–6pm | opposite the Ritsurin-koen | tel. 08 78 31 67 79 | Budget)*.

Continue by train from Ritsurin-koen station to Mount Yashima with spectacular views of the inland lake and the impressive Seto-Ohashi Bridge. At the foot of Yashima is the museum village of ❷ **Shikoku Mura** *(daily 8.30am–5.30pm | admission 800 ¥)* with 33 traditional buildings from Shikoku and an exhibition building designed by the well-known architect Tadao Ando.

From Yashima there is a train to rocky Mount Goken with the ❸ **Isamu Noguchi Garden Museum** *(guided tours Tue, Thu, Sat only at 10am, 1pm and 3pm by prior booking |*

admission 2160 ¥ | tel. 08 78 70 15 00 | www.noguchi.org/museum/japan) with works by the Japanese-American sculptor and designer Isamu Noguchi. This is a truly unique ensemble of 150 sculptures, residence, studio, garden and surroundings. Stay at the central JR Hotel **④ Clement Takamatsu** *(300 rooms | 1-1 Hamanocho | tel. 0 87 81 11 11 | www.jrclement.co.jp/en | Moderate)* with lovely views of the inland sea.

Next day, **an hour's train ride will see you in ⑤ Kotohira**. It's 785 stone steps up to the **Kompirasan**, the island's main Shinto shrine. It is dedicated to the god of sailors and seafaring. The challenging ascent (approx. 45 min) is rewarded with fabulous views of the Sanuki plain and fabulous shrine.

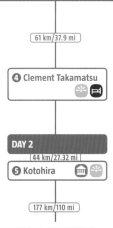

61 km/37.9 mi

④ Clement Takamatsu

DAY 2

44 km/27.32 mi

⑤ Kotohira

177 km/110 mi

Green tea is a must with a session at the Dogo Onsen Honkan

Afterwards take the train that will get you to ⑥ Matsuyama, the island's biggest town, in 2½ hours. It has a **castle** and several shrines that are worth visiting. 4 km/2.5 mi to the north-east is **⑦ Dogo Onsen**, Japan's oldest and most prominent thermal spa resort that is also visited by the imperial family. **It's only four minutes on**

⑥ Matsuyama

5 km/3.1 mi

⑦ Dogo Onsen

251 km/156 mi

119

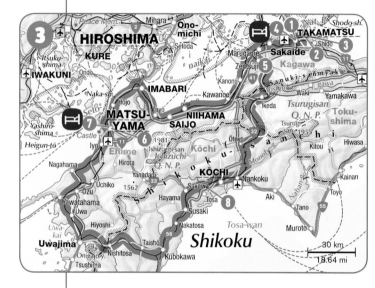

foot from the station to the town's main attraction, the three-storey **Dogo Onsen Honkan**, built in 1894 *(daily 6am–11pm | admission 410–1550 ¥)* with a communal pool and fabulous roof. The bathhouse is said to have been the inspiration behind Hayao Miyazaki's popular animation "Spirited Away". Enjoy a bath in a traditional atmosphere and, depending on the admission fee, a cup of green tea, a snack and a visit to the imperial family's private tract.

You'll encounter an INSIDER TIP unusual photo motif **on the way from the Dogo Onsen Honkan to the station:** visitors often stroll around a 250 m/820 ft shopping arcade in *yukata* robes. Just 200 m/656 ft from the station, check in to the traditionally elegant **Hotel Funaya** *(58 rooms | tel. 08 99 47 02 78 | www.dogo-funaya.co.jp | Expensive)* and enjoy an evening meal in its excellent restaurant.

DAY 3

Next morning, continue even further south by train: to the semi-tropical prefecture of **Kochi**, where the spectacular coast spans a wide arch between two rugged promontories. The striking coastal landscape with national parks, bays and beaches is ideal for outdoor activities such as kayaking, surfing and whale watching.

The area around **Cape Ashizuri** is excellent for watching whales and dolphins, who come there all year round to enjoy the shoals of fish. Three- to four-hour boat trips are offered from several ports in ❽ **Tosa Shimizu** (*daily departure 1pm | ticket 5000 ¥ | www.shimizu-kankou. com.e.cp.hp.transer.com*). **The train will have you back in ❶ Takamatsu in three hours**.

❽ Tosa Shimizu

179 km/111 mi

❶ Takamatsu

---

④ HOLY PILGRIMAGE

START: ❶ Kii-Tanabe END: ❽ Yunomine	3 days Actual walking time 12 hours
Distance: ➡ 45 km/28 mi	Level of difficulty: difficult

COSTS: Accommodation, meals, admissions approx. 55,000 yen per person
WHAT TO PACK: Hiking shoes or boots, sunscreen, rain jacket, water

IMPORTANT TIPS: The JR Limited Express goes to ❶ **Kii-Tanabe** from Osaka. It's best to book overnight accommodation in advance. The walk is challenging, and difficult in places.

The Kii peninsula is one of Japan's most mystical places. The almost 90,000 shrines and temples in its bamboo woods and coastal strips have been linked for more than 1000 years by a network of pilgrim paths. A three-day hike of the famous Nakahechi route is a unique spiritual, cultural and sporting experience.

Start on the coast in ❶ **Kii-Tanabe**. As you will be setting off early on the hike, it's best to spend the night before at the **Altier Hotel** (*49 rooms | tel. 0739811111 | www.altier hotel.com | Budget*), which is only 250 m/820 ft from the station. Its rooms are basic but spacious, with views of the sea or city.

In the morning the bus leaves for ❷ Takijiri-oji, the spiritual entrance to the holy Kumano Mountains. **From there, you continue on foot along the Nakahechi path (signposted) for about 13 km/8.1 mi to Chikatsuyu.** The first section consists of forest paths interspersed by some high steps and cobbles, and lovely views of ❸ **Takahara**, the "Village in the Mist", so called because the mountain landscape is often shrouded in mist. The attraction of this former postal station is colourful **Takahara Kumano-jin-ja**, one of the oldest shrines in the region in the midst

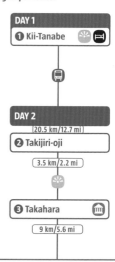

DAY 1
❶ Kii-Tanabe

DAY 2
20.5 km/12.7 mi
❷ Takijiri-oji
3.5 km/2.2 mi
❸ Takahara
9 km/5.6 mi

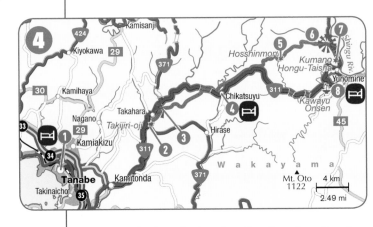

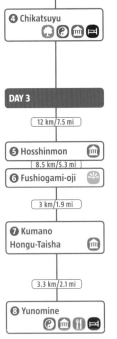

④ Chikatsuyu

---

of vast camphor trees. **From there the route continues to the village of ④ Chikatsuyu** with the eponymous shrine. At the Ryokan **Minshuku Chikatsuyu** *(6 rooms | www.kumano-travel.com | Budget)*, which is beside the river and has a hot spring, guests stay in tatami rooms (shared bathroom and toilet).

DAY 3

12 km/7.5 mi

⑤ Hosshinmon

8.5 km/5.3 mi

⑥ Fushiogami-oji

3 km/1.9 mi

⑦ Kumano Hongu-Taisha

3.3 km/2.1 mi

⑧ Yunomine

The hike continues on day 3 **across 25 km/15.5 mi of mountainous terrain**, past lots of minor shrines, the *ojis*. The Japanese pray here for inner peace and for other wishes and aims to come true. Memorable stops along the way are the **⑤ Hosshinmon** (Gateway to Enlightenment) and the lookout point **⑥ Fushiogami-oji** with far-reaching views of the former **Hongu-Taisha** estate in the valley below. It was destroyed in a massive flood in 1889. The current shrine is now further inland, but its torii (the biggest one in Japan) is on the original site. **The way to the "new" main Shinto shrine ⑦ Kumano Hongu-Taisha is up a very steep tree-lined stairway.** All the pilgrim paths converge here in a star.

The Dainichi-goe path (some signs are in English) gets you to the spa resort ⑧ Yunomine in about an hour. Its bathhouses, and above all the healing water, are much appreciated all over Japan. INSIDER TIP Relax in complete privacy at the **Tsuboyu onsen** *(daily 6am–9.30pm | admission 770 ¥ for 30 min and maximum 2 people | Hongu | tel. 07 35 42 00 74 | www.tb-kumano.jp/en/onsen/ yunomine)*. Pilgrims were already washing themselves at this tiny bathhouse 1800 years ago; today it's a Unesco

---

World Heritage Site. The hot mineral water is said to cure any disease.

End your walk with an evening meal at the Ryokan **Min-shuki Kuraya** *(4 rooms | book at www.tb-kumano.jp/en | Budget)*, where you will spend the night. Next morning, a bus will take you from here back to the starting point at Kii-Tanabe in 90 minutes.

⑤ WILD HOKKAIDO

START: ❶ Sapporo END: ❿ Sounkyo Gorge	5 days Driving time 20 hours
Distance: ➡ 1038 km/645 mi	

COSTS: Hire car, fuel, accommodation, meals, tour guide approx. 120,000 yen per person
WHAT TO PACK: Hiking shoes or boots, swimming things, non-skid bathing shoes, whistle (because of the bears in the National Park)

IMPORTANT TIPS: When hiring a car, be sure to get a user-friendly or English-speaking satnav system.
❹ **Shiretoko Goko:** For conservation reasons, during peak season (May to July), the paths may only be used by prior booking and with guides *(approx. 5000 ¥ | www.goko.go.jp/ fivelakes)*. Best time to go May to October. Some areas are closed in winter.

In the language of the indigenous Ainu, the north-east tip of Hokkaido means „End of the world". For nature lovers, the Shiretoko National Park of the Sea of Okhotsk is an unspoilt hikers' paradise with numerous waterfalls, hot springs and active volcanoes.

From ❶ **Sapporo, continue along developed road for about five hours to** ❷ **Abashiri**, the gateway to the **Shiretoko** National Park *(visitor information: tel. 052 445 849)*. Due to the unique flora and fauna (brown bears and sea eagles), the region and adjoining marine reserve were declared a Unesco World Heritage Site in 2005. Stay at the **Abashiri Kankou Hotel** *(110 rooms | tel. 0152 2121 | breezbay-group.com/abashiri-kh | Budget)*, which is right beside Lake Abashiri and offers wonderful panoramic views. A good way to end the day is in a relaxing bath in one of the hotel's onsens (both indoors and outdoors). **The coastal road takes you north-east to** ❸ **Utoro**. From

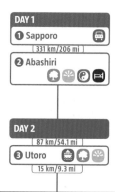

DAY 1
❶ Sapporo
331 km/206 mi
❷ Abashiri

DAY 2
87 km/54.1 mi
❸ Utoro
15 km/9.3 mi

the end of April until October, there are six boat trips a day from the harbour, e.g. **Aurora Ships** *(duration 90 min | ticket 3100 ¥ | www.ms-aurora.com/shiretoko/en)* along the rocky coast with its breathtaking cliffs, waterfalls and rocks.

And even more water after the boat ride. To get to the five lakes of Shiretoko with fabulous views of unspoilt landscapes, **take the main road to the Shiretoko Nature Centre, then drive another 10 km/6.2 mi to the car park at the ④ Shiretoko Goko visitor centre. There's an 800 m/ 2625 ft long wooden walkway to the first lake.** You will need a briefing (500 ¥) for all other hikes. Not to be missed: a INSIDER TIP dip in the warm waterfalls of the ⑤ **Kamui Wakka no Taki** that bubble away a further 10 km/ 6.2 mi along the gravel track.

Drive for 50 minutes and spend two nights near the hot springs of ⑥ **Iwaobetsu Onsen** *(closed in winter)* at the **Hotel Chinohate** *(41 rooms | tel. 0152 24 23 31 | Moderate)*.

The trail up to ⑦ **Rausu-dake (1660 m/5446 ft),** the highest and wildest peak of the chain of volcanoes in the middle of the park, starts outside the hotel. Allow about eight hours for the challenging ascent and return. **There's**

④ Shiretoko Goko

〔 28 km/17.4 mi 〕

⑤ Kamui Wakka no Taki

〔 17.5 km/10.9 mi 〕

⑥ Iwaobetsu Onsen

DAY 3

〔 7 km/4.4 mi 〕

⑦ Rausu-dake

Hike to the rocky peak of Rausu-dake: challenging ascent, unique views

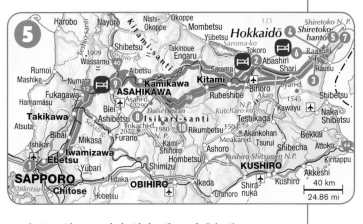

a short stretch over rocks just below the peak. Enjoy the fabulous views at the top of the island chain of the southern Kuril Islands, object of dispute between Russia and Japan.

On the way back to Sapporo, stop at ⑧ Daisetsuzan National Park *(www.daisetsuzan.or.jp/english)*, Japan's biggest national park spanning 888 mi² in the centre of Hokkaido – an unspoilt area with active volcanoes and

alpine meadows, hot springs and forests. The highest peak in the impressive mountain chain known as the „Roof over Hokkaido" is Mount Asahi (2290 m/7513 ft). Spend the night in ⑨ **Asahikawa**, the second biggest town in Hokkaido, at the Ryokan **Senshoen** *(18 rooms | tel. 0166 615154 | www.sensyoen.co.jp/index.php | Moderate)*, a luxurious guest house with hot springs as well as excellent cuisine.

From Asahikawa, it's worth taking a day trip to the 24-km/14.9-mi ⑩ **Sounkyo Gorge** with its fabulous waterfalls. It takes about three hours to drive back from Asahikawa to Sapporo.

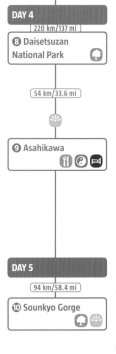

DAY 4

220 km/137 mi

⑧ Daisetsuzan National Park 🌲

54 km/33.6 mi

⑨ Asahikawa 🍴 ☕ 🛏

DAY 5

94 km/58.4 mi

⑩ Sounkyo Gorge 🌲 🌸

SPORTS & ACTIVITIES

Jogging or cycle paths and gyms are almost everywhere. Otherwise, it is slightly more difficult –and usually more expensive – to organise sporting and cultural activities than in other countries (especially golf and tennis). The typical Japanese hobbies require years of training.

For martial arts fans, several organisation also welcome foreigners, although they will be asked to pay a registration or monthly fee.

Incidentally, the country that has hosted three Olympic Games and Asia's first FIFA World Cup is crazy about baseball. Events in the two leagues of the professional Japanese teams are followed with virtually fanatical devotion, with the excitement almost beyond endurance when Japanese stars play in the US professional league.

BEACHES & SURFING

Although Japan is an elongated island kingdom, visitors will usually search in vain for a tropical paradise and well-tended beaches. But today there are several recreation areas where surfers, canoeists and swimmers will find what makes them happy. The most popular centres of the Tokyoans include the Shonan beaches in Kamakura, around 50 km/31.1 mi from Tokyo and easy to get to by train.

The Pacific Ocean is relatively calm, and also suitable for novice surfers. The bathing season runs from 1 July until 31 August. There are parties everywhere

Bathing in a hot spring and cycling through one of the most exciting cities in the world – how to experience Japan differently

in summer. Professional surfers head to the Izu peninsula and the Shirahama beaches, which are popular with all water sports lovers. Convenient train connections from Tokyo take about 3 hours. Fabulous surfing conditions and lovely beaches can be found on the southern islands of Ishigaki and Ogasawara, although they are around 2000 km/ 1243 mi from Tokyo and can only be reached by air or boat (26 hours from Tokyo). Information: *www.outdoor japan.com*

CYCLING

Away from the big cities, the islands Hokkaido, Kyushu and Shikoku and less densely populated regions on Honshu, offer lots of lovely countryside and destinations for extensive tours. Bicycles can be hired from the railway stations for between 500 ¥ and 1500 ¥ a day, and returned to the nearest one at the end of it. Cyclists are not so well tolerated in the major cities. The first cycle paths are being built in Tokyo, but otherwise it is very tiring to battle one's way through the pedestrians. Cyclists move around the imperial palace entirely without stress on Sundays, when several broad streets in the spacious area are reserved for recreational athletes, who can borrow a bicycle free of charge from the *Imperial Cycling Station (behind the Babasakimon Gate)*. Guided tours of Tokyo are offered in English on Tuesdays, Thursdays, Saturdays and Sundays and on request by the *Tokyo Great Cycling Tour Office (tel. 03 45 90 29 95 | www.tokyocycling.jp)*. The tour, which lasts about six hours, including bicycle, guide, insurance and a packed lunch costs 10,000 ¥.

The bicycle is the best way to explore Kyoto. *Kyoto Cycling Tour Project (from 5900 ¥ | tel. 075 3 54 36 36 | www.kctp. net/en)* offers seven themed tours of between three and eight hours, as well as a cookery course.

HIKING

Organised "hikes" are often a joke in Japan: you get off the bus, stroll 300 m/ 1000 ft to a famous lookout point or waterfall, walk around the souvenir stands, and then head back to the bus. And yet the country, which is 80 percent mountains, has such terrific possibilities (see p. 116 and p. 121). Usually only pilgrims on spiritual tours move at a sportier pace, perhaps to the 88 temples on Shikoku or to the holy mountains in Wakayama. Prepare thoroughly for an individual hike, because the paths are usually poorly signposted, and mostly in Japanese. The Kamikochi Mountains in the Japanese Alps are quite unspoilt, with lots of paths and trails *(information: tel. 02 63 95 24 33 | www.kamikochi.or.jp/ english)*.

JUDO

Japan's most famous martial art goes back to a form a self-defence that was practised by the Samurai. The idea is that the opponent's strength is to be used to one's own advantage for grips and throws. The most famous judo ("gentle way") school is *Kodokan* in Tokyo. *Registration fee 5000 ¥ | around 8000 ¥ a month (watching from the gallery is free) | International department tel. 03 38 18 41 72 | www.kod okan.org*

KENDO

Today, traditional sword fighting is practised as a sport at many schools. The weapon is a bamboo sword, and players wear a mask, breastplate and gloves, which are also the opponent's targets. Players can practice at the famous hall, *Tokyo Budokan. 300 ¥ per practice session, 20 units 6000 ¥ | Information: All Nippon Kendo Federation | tel. 03 32 11 58 04 | www.kendo-fik.org*

ONSEN

These hot springs are down to Japan's volcanic origins. The temperature of the water, which is often sulphurous, is between 40 and 60 degrees. The Japanese swear by its health benefits. As more and more people, almost always segregated by gender, enter the pools, the rules absolutely must be observed. Bathers enter the bathing room naked after washing themselves thoroughly with plenty of soap and shampoo under a shower with a wooden ladle that is filled at the tap. Only then may they immerse themselves in the water. There are lots of lovely onsen in the Hakone region at the foot of Mount Fuji.

SKI & SNOWBOARDING

Japan is one of the snowiest countries in the world, with around 700 skiing regions. Winter sports enthusiasts will find fabulous conditions on the island of Hokkaido, which has around five months of powder snow every year, and – unlike other centres – a number of cross-country tracks. Information on ski slopes near Sapporo: *www.welcome. city.sapporo.jp.*

Japan's biggest ski resort *Shiga Kogen (www.ski-resorts-japan.com/shiga-ko gen)* with around 70 lifts is 90 minutes from Tokyo by fast train. For the most challenging Olympic run, head for the Hakuba Valley at 2000 m/6562 ft. The ski season here ends in early May. The ten Hakuba resorts that are considered the top destinations for complete snow freaks include *Happo-One*, which – like Hokkaido – is extremely welcoming to foreigners. *www.snowjapan.com* offers an overview of all the centres with maps, details of the lifts, prices, the lengths of the runs and levels of difficulty, and weather forecasts. You can see the regions on the ski and snowboard website *www.snowjapan.tv.*

SUMO

Nippon's oldest national sport, allegedly 2000 years old, is easy to understand. Two heavily overweight, almost naked giants bang into each other, and the first one to make the other leave the ring or fall over is the winner. It rarely takes longer than three minutes (information at *www.sumo.or.jp/eng/index. html*). The noise level beats that of many discos, and with a little luck you can not only admire the obese demi-gods close up, but even touch them – which is said

Kendo fighters in action

to transfer their strength to the one touching them. There is a strict hierarchy. After any of the six annual tournaments, the fighters may be promoted or demoted. Only grand masters retain their title of *Yokosuna* for life, and most usually start their own school or take over another one when their careers are over. *Visits possible after booking, e.g. in Dewanoumibeyam in Tokyo | tel. 03 36 32 49 20*

TRAVEL WITH KIDS

There are no problems with taking children into restaurant, hotels or on public transport. However, the narrow towns, busy streets and few leisure activities are not always ideal for little ones. Consult the website *www.tokyowithkids.com* for information on festivals and park activities for children.

EASTERN AND CENTRAL JAPAN

EDO TOKYO OPEN AIR ARCHITECTURAL MUSEUM (151 D4) (*∅ G7*)

Little children can rush around in the open-air at Tokyo's Koganei Park, while older ones will enjoy finding out what life in Tokyo used to be like in authentic houses, public baths and shops. Noodle restaurants, special exhibitions and presentations will turn a family day out into an experience. *Tue–Sun April–Sep 9.30am–5.30pm, Oct–March 9.30am–4.30pm | Admission 400¥, children 200¥ | tel. 042 3 88 33 00 | www.tatemonoen.jp/english*

INSIDER TIP **KIDZANIA** (U F5) (*∅ f5*)

A thrill for children between 2 and 15 years of age with 90 different activities. In Tokyo's biggest playroom, youngster can play at 50 different jobs and professions, under professional supervision, dressed in original Japanese company uniforms. The concept is extremely popular because it is new, exciting and informative – "edutainment" at its very best. *Daily 9am–3pm and 4pm–9pm | Admission based on age and day between 2900¥ and 4900¥ | tel. 03 35 36 84 05 | Booking essential at www.kidzania.jp/tokyo/en*

TOKYO DISNEYLAND (151 D4) (*∅ G7*)

Japan's favourite family destination is a copy of the Californian original, but also has the world's first sea theme park, *Tokyo Disney Sea Park*. At weekends and public holidays, you might have to queue for up to two hours for some of the 23 attractions. *Mon–Fri 9am–10pm, Sat/Sun 8am–10pm | Day ticket for both theme parks 6900¥, children to age 11 4500¥ | the quickest way to get there is on the JR Keiyo line to Maihama, and there are shuttle buses from Tokyo main station (Tokyo Station, Yaesu exit) | tel. 045 3 30 52 11 | www.tokyodisneyresort.co.jp/en*

NORTHERN JAPAN

RUSUTSU RESORT (148 C3) (*∅ H3*)

Japan's biggest leisure park is on Lake Toya, and is a vast complex of concrete

The Japanese love theme parks: they offer fun and games for children and their parents – and absolutely no language barriers

and Japanese kitsch. One of the restaurants for example is called Oktoberfest, and in the middle of the hotel are a children's merry-go-round, a Christmas shop and a World of Pokémon. Children will love the roller-coaster goose bumps they get on the more than 60 rides, and the fantasy worlds of stuffed animals and flying carpets. Or the sporting offers such as ski runs, dog sled rides, the super pool and horse trekking. *Daily 9am–5pm | Day ticket 4950 ¥, children (up to age 12) 3950 ¥, younger 1200 ¥ | Rusutsu-mura | tel. 0136 46 31 11 | en.rusutsu.co.jp*

WESTERN JAPAN

AQUARIUM KAIYUKAN ●
(153 F3) (*ᗯ E8*)

Eye to eye with the inhabitants of the seas in Osaka Tempozan: The Kaiyukan Aquarium is one of the biggest of its kind in the world. It contains almost all the species that live in the Pacific. More

than 35,000 different creatures, including huge whale sharks, can be observed on 14 levels. *Daily 10am–8pm | Admission 2300 ¥, children 600–1200 ¥ | tel. 06 65 76 55 01 | www.kaiyukan.com/language/eng*

UMINONAKAMICHI SEASIDE PARK
(152 B4) (*ᗯ B8*)

The biggest theme park in western Japan has the "Sunshine Pool", which consists of a total of six pools (but which are only open from mid-July until the end of August), large trampolines, play areas, a Ferris wheel and lots of food stands. Seasonal events all year round, and Aquarium Marine World is also worth a visit. *March–Oct 9.30am–5.30pm, Nov–Feb 9.30am–5pm | Admission 410 ¥, children 80 ¥ | Oaza Saitozakic | tel. 0926 03 11 11 | yokanavi.com/eg/theme/detail/85*

FESTIVALS & EVENTS

If a public holiday falls on a weekend, people have the Monday off instead. The main holiday and travel times (with over-full public transport) are the *Golden Week* at the beginning of May, the *Obon* festival in the middle of August for commemorating one's ancestors, and the Emperor's Birthday on 23 December, when the imperial family steps out onto a palace balcony.

FESTIVALS & EVENTS

JANUARY

Turn of the Year (31 Dec–3 Jan): People visit shrines, relations and business partners, gift each other and eat lots of food.
2nd Sun in Jan: INSIDER TIP ▸ ***Coming of Age Day:*** Young people proceed through the streets dressed in fabulous clothes.

FEBRUARY

Setsubun (3 Feb): In temples and shrines, people throw beans into the air accompanied by the words "Demons out! Luck in!".
⭐ ***Snow Festival (1st week of February)*** In Odori Park at Sapporo, with lots of ice status of famous buildings and fantasy figures. www.snowfes.com
INSIDER TIP ▸ ***Naked Festival (3rd Sat):*** Saidai-ji temple near Okayama celebrates a cleansing ritual at which young men, clad only in a loincloth, try to catch willow strips thrown by priests into the darkness.

MARCH/APRIL

Dolls' Festival (3 March): Little girls are given dolls representing the old court.
Cherry Blossom (end March/beg. April): Folk festival with food, drink and song. The biggest sakura party (*sakura* means cherry blossom) is held in Tokyo's Ueno Park.

MAY

5 May*: Boys' Day*: Families with sons hang out bamboo sticks with colourful fabric as a symbol of resistance and endurance.
INSIDER TIP ▸ ***Sanja Festival (16–18 May):*** Around 80 portable shrines are carried into Tokyo, to the accompaniment of drums and shouts.
Toshugu Festival in Nikko (17–18 May): Thousands of men on horseback dressed as Samurai and armed with bows and arrows escort portable shrines.

JULY

Gion Matsuri in Kyoto (17 July): Festival procession of geishas on wonderful floats ***Sumida*** and ***Rainbow Festival*** in Tokyo ***(3rd/4th Sat)*** with fireworks beside the Sumida River

Japan's biggest folk festival is in the spring, its popularity probably only matched by the Snow Festival in February

AUGUST

Nebuta Matsuri (2–7 Aug): floats process through Aomori.

Fuji Rock Festival (beg. Aug) in Naeba: despite the admission being over 39,000 yen, it is a magnet for 250,000 fans

Lantern Festival of Kasuga Shrine in Nara (15 Aug): 3000 lanterns light the way to the shrine.

Obon (around 15 Aug), according to Buddhist belief, when one's ancestors return.

OCTOBER

Jidai Matsuri in Kyoto (22 Oct): Commemorates the founding of the town in 794; procession of people in historic costumes

NOVEMBER

INSIDER TIP **Shichi-Go-San (15 Nov):** At this children's festival, beautifully dressed girls aged 3 and 7, and little boys aged 5, pray for blessings at temples or shrines. Best seen at the Meiji shrine in Tokyo

PUBLIC HOLIDAYS

1 Jan	New Year's Day
2nd Sun in Jan	Coming of Age Day
11 Feb	National Foundation Day
20/21 March	Spring Equinox
29 April	Showa Day
3 May	Constitution Memorial Day
4 May	Greenery Day
5 May	Boys' Day
20 July	Sea Day
11 Aug	Mountain Day
15 Sep	Respect for the Aged Day
23/24 Sep	September/ Autumn Equinox
2nd Mon in Oct	Sports Day
3 Nov	Culture Day
23 Nov	Labour Thanksgiving Day
23 Dec	Emperor's Birthday

LINKS, BLOGS, APPS & MORE

www.japan-guide.com Highly informative travel portal in English with current updates, photos and new services. Also finds pen friends

www.tokyofoodlife.com Exciting tips for favourite Japanese dishes and the right restaurants. Plus reports on dinner boat trips on Tokyo's Sumida River and the relief action provided by a successful Italian restaurant owner in the disaster region

web-japan.org/links A comprehensive list of useful websites on topics such as politics, economy, culture, travel, sports, media etc.

japanvisitor.blogspot.de Hotel recommendations and more for Tokyo, Osaka, Nagoya and Kyoto

www.geishablog.com This Japan blog provides information on everything that is exciting about this country and its innovative products: mangas and fashion, music, shopping and much more (in English)

www.wordpress.tokyotimes.org Photographer Lee Chapman reports with pictures and English texts on very different aspects of his chosen home Tokyo

www.virtualtourist.com/asia/japan Experiences and tips from people who have been to Japan for any life situation

www.budgetyourtrip.com/japan For a good idea of costs for all sorts of things, plus lots of travel tips

Regardless of whether you are still preparing your trip or already in Japan: these addresses will provide you with more information, videos and networks to make your holiday even more enjoyable

short.travel/jap1 „Hayaku – A Time Lapse Journey Through Japan" is an artistic, emotional video by Bred Kremer

short.travel/jap2 The video channel of the Japanese tourist organisation JNTO contains reports on Japanese regions, interviews and animes, many of them with English subtitles

www.nhk.or.jp/kawaii-i For all those who like things kawaii, that is cute, Japan's public law TV channel offers the latest trends with tips and analyses of the various subcultures, from Lolita and Gyaru to Sweet Cherry, on "Kawaii International"

Japan Map (itsumo NAVI) Easy, clear navigation system by Zenrin DataCom (with 400,000 towns) for iPhone and iPad

line One of the most frequently loaded apps in Japan for social networks. Works for no charge. A large fan community loves the funny stickers that brighten up photos

GuruNavi The best app for finding a restaurant. Listed by the area where you are, by type of cuisine or by budget. Often also offers discounts or free drinks

Triposo Ideal for orientation in Tokyo, Osaka and Kyoto, with maps and categories (museums, architecture, hiking etc.). Other feature: Travel Dashboard with currency converter, weather and useful Japanese expressions. For iPhone, iPad and Android

Imiwa Japanese dictionary, aids understanding. For iPhone and iPad

TRAVEL TIPS

ADDRESSES

Finding an address in Japan is a tremendous challenge, even for the Japanese. The country is not big on street names. Let's assume you're looking for 5-4-13 Denenchofu, Ota-ku, Tokyo. This is how to get there: look for house no. 13 in block 4 of the 5th rayon in the district of Denenchofu in the Tokyo borough of Ota. But that's not to say that house no. 13 is located between no. 12 and 14; it could be somewhere entirely different. Taxi drivers also often despair.

The best solution is to take a detailed route sketch and phone number that the driver can call if necessary. In large towns and cities, the borough can provide basic orientation, so we have dispensed with the addresses in this book, and instead provide the phone numbers and/or districts.

RESPONSIBLE TRAVEL

It doesn't take a lot to be environmentally friendly whilst travelling. Don't just think about your carbon footprint whilst flying to and from your holiday destination but also about how you can protect nature and culture abroad. As a tourist it is especially important to respect nature, look out for local products, cycle instead of driving, save water and much more. If you would like to find out more about eco-tourism please visit: www.ecotourism.org

ARRIVAL

There are direct scheduled flights from London (e.g. British Airways, Japan Airlines, ANA) and Frankfurt (Lufthansa, All Nippon Airways and Japan Airlines). The flights from Europe go to Tokyo-Haneda, Tokyo-Narita, Kansai/Osaka and Nagoya. There are also direct flights from different airports in the United States to Tokyo and Osaka (Japan Airlines).

The quickest way from Narita to Tokyo city centre is by Narita Express (NEX) to Tokyo Station *(main station | travel time 53min | 3020 ¥ in second class | www.jreast.co.jp./e)*. You should arrange tickets and seat reservations in advance. If you have a lot of luggage, it is recommended to use the airport limousine *(3000 ¥)* to the City Terminal or all the major hotels in Tokyo. At peak times, the travel time may far exceed the average time of 70 min. The same applies to arrivals at Kansai airport in the Bay of Osaka. Take care with taxis: they may cost 25,000 ¥, and the police warn against black private taxis for insurance reasons. The Japanese use delivery companies for their luggage, which are easy to find at the airports. They will deliver on the same day for 1600 ¥ per item. However, it can be difficult to arrange this service if you don't speak Japanese.

Travelling by Trans-Siberian Railway (to Vladivostok) and ferry to Niigata is as charming as it is expensive. Furthermore, it is difficult to arrange without a travel agent (the travel time is 10 days).

From arrival to weather

Holiday from start to finish: the most important addresses and information for your trip to Japan

BANKS & CHANGING MONEY

It is best to change money at the airport or in a hotel. Money can also be changed in branches of any major bank (they are usually opened Mon–Fri, 9am–3pm), at some main post offices in cities and in department stores (including traveller's cheques). Hotels and many restaurants in cities will accept credit cards. But you will have to use cash in smaller shops and the provinces. You can withdraw cash using a credit charge for a fee (better check in advance, which fees are charged by your bank or credit institute). International cash machines are increasingly available (also in English).

CAMPING

There are about 2800 official campsites (including tent and bungalow hire), many of which are only open in July and August. JNTO has a detailed INSIDERTIP Camping in Japan brochure. The sites are often overfull during holidays and at weekends.

CLIMATE, WHEN TO GO

The pleasantest times are spring – ideally at cherry blossom time in March/April – and autumn (especially November/early December) with mild temperatures and glorious autumn foliage. Avoid going between June and August because it rains a lot and is very humid. In winter, it can be very cold with heavy snow on Hokkaido, in northern Honshu and in the mountains.

COMMUNICATING

An individual stay can be very difficult with no Japanese language skills. Although English has been a compulsory subject in schools for many years, most Japanese avoid speaking a foreign language. However, this reticence can be overcome with friendliness and patience.

CURRENCY CONVERTER

£	Yen	Yen	£
10	1420	100	0.70
25	3550	200	1.40
70	9940	300	2.10
100	14,200	450	3.15
125	17,750	700	4.90
200	28,400	1000	7
300	42,600	3500	24.50
425	60,350	5000	35
500	71,000	10,000	70

$	Yen	Yen	$
10	1110	100	0.90
25	2775	200	1.80
70	7770	300	2.70
100	11,100	450	4.05
125	13,875	700	6.30
200	22,200	1000	9
300	33,300	3500	31.50
425	47,175	5000	45
500	55,500	10,000	90

For current exchange rates see www.xe.com

CONSULATES & EMBASSIES

BRITISH EMBASSY TOKYO
Ichiban-cho, Chiyoda-ku | tel. 03 52 11

11 00 | www.gov.uk.government/world/organisations/british-embassy-tokyo

BRITISH CONSULATE GENERAL OSAKA

Bakuro-machi, Chuo-ku | tel. 06 61 20 56 00 | www.gov.uk/government/world/organisations/british-consulate-general-osaka

U.S. EMBASSY TOKYO

Aka-saka, Minato-ku | tel. 03 32 24 50 00 | www.jp.usembassy.gov

CUSTOMS

Visitors may import three bottles of alcoholic drinks, 400 cigarettes, 100 cigars or 500 g tobacco, 60 g perfume and gifts worth up to 200,000 ¥ into Japan, but no meat or meat products. The valid quarantine rules apply if you wish to bring plants or animals with you. When returning home to the UK, there is no duty on goods worth up to 390 £ (800 US$ for the US). Some other allowances: 200 cigarettes or 100 cigarillos or 50 cigars or 250 g tobacco and 1 l spirits. More information about customs regulations at *www.gov.uk/duty-free-goods/arrivals-from-outside-the-eu* and *www.cbp.gov/travel/us-citizens.*

DOMESTIC FLIGHTS

Domestic flights are operated mainly by Japan Airlines and All Nippon Airways. There are also niche providers on some routes. Information from travel agents and at *www.jal.com, www.anaskyweb.com.*

DRIVING

Car hire is absolutely not recommended. An international driving licence will not be recognised without an official translation (by the relevant embassy), and the original plus a certified copy both have to be presented. Then there are the exorbitant tolls and parking fees. The Japanese drive on the left side of the road.

EARTHQUAKE

In the event of an earthquake, you must follow the official instructions or, in the event of doubt, the movements of most local residents. Whatever you do, stay calm. If you are in a hotel stay on the floor and find a relatively safe spot, such as a doorway or under a table. Under no circumstances should you use a lift. If outside, find a place where nothing can fall over or on you. Do not take any items that could be a hindrance on your escape.

ELECTRICITY

110 volt a.c. Japanese electrical plugs have two non-polarized pins. We recommend purchasing a travel adapter before you leave.

EMERGENCY SERVICES

Police: *tel. 110,* in English *03 35 01 01 10;* Fire/emergency doctor: *tel. 119;* Japan Helpline: *tel. 0570 00 09 11*

HEALTH

No specific vaccinations are required for a journey to Japan. But you should make sure to bring any necessary medication with you from home. In an emergency, go to the *Tokyo Medical & Surgical Clinic (Mori Building 32 | Shiba Koen | tel. 03 34 36 30 28,* only in urgent emergencies: *tel. 03 34 32 61 34).*

All of the staff at this clinic speak English. English is also spoken at *St. Luke's Hospital and Clinic (Tokyo, Chuo | tel. 03 35 41 51 51)*.

IMMIGRATION

A passport that is valid for the duration of the visit is required. British and US-American citizens can enter Japan as a visitor for up to 90 days without a visa (you will receive a 90-day visa on arrival, which is extendable for a further 3 month for citizens of the United Kingdom). Please note that you may need to provide evidence of a return/onward ticket.

INFORMATION IN JAPAN

The English information service of the Japan National Tourism Organization (JNTO) will help with travel arrangements *(Tokyo: daily 9am–5pm | Shin-Tokyo Building 1st Floor | tel. 03 32 01 33 31)*. There are also 525 *Tourist Information Centers (TIC)* in Japan, all at *www.jnto.go.jp/eng*.

INFORMATION BEFORE YOU TRAVEL

JAPAN NATIONAL TOURISM ORGANIZATION (JNTO)
The *Japan National Tourism Organization* send out brochures that help to save money, for instance for the reasonably-priced "Welcome Inns". *www.jnto.go.jp*

JAPAN TRAVEL BUREAU
You can also obtain the *Japan Rail Pass* here.
3rd floor, No. 1 Farriers Yard, 77–85 Fulham Palace Rd., London | tel. 020 82 37 16 00 | www.jtbuk.com

BUDGETING

Coffee	2.65 £/3.35 $
	for one cup in a café
Beer	3.50 £/4.50 $
	for a small glass
Noodle soup	4.40 £/5.60 $
	for a basic soup
Museum	4.40 £/5.60 $
	for admission
Fans	22 £/28 $
	for a souvenir fan
Underground	0.90 £/1.10 $
	for one ticket (one way)

INTERNET ACCESS & WIFI

Internet cafés are everywhere, and there are terminals in all the major hotels, libraries and town halls. Free WIFI is becoming more common, especially in cafés and small guesthouses. Most of the major hotels charge the usual international prices. Internet access is only available on trains and at stations from Japanese providers and for a fee. Most Japanese apps are only available in that language. Expect high roaming charges if using European providers for apps and Internet.

MEDIA

There are two daily newspapers in English, "Japan Times" and "Japan News". Dining and event tips are provided in the free magazines "Metropolis", "J Select", "Tokyo Classified" and "Kansai Time Out" (obtainable in hotels, supermarkets and book stores). International hotels usually broadcast English satellite TV. You can also watch the main evening news programme in English on the public-law channel using two-channel sound.

PHONE & MOBILE PHONE

To phone Japan from the United Kingdom, dial 0081 (from the United States: 01181), then the dial code omitting the first 0, and then the subscriber number.

To make a foreign call from Japan, first dial a phone company (e.g. 001 for KDDI or 0041 for Nicon Telecom), then the national code (UK 44, US 1), then the dial code without the 0, and the subscriber number.

KDDI *credit phones* in hotels and at airports accept international credit cards. The operator number is 0051.

The Japanese government set up the travel phone for tourists. This telephone service (in English) helps if you are in difficulty or need information. From a public phone, insert 10 ¥, dial 106 and ask in English for a collect call with *TIC (collect call TIC)*.

For information on using a mobile phone in Japan please go to www.*japan-guide.com*. Several companies rent out mobile phones to foreign tourists, and if booked in advance will ensure they are at the hotel or airport punctually *(www.rentafonejapan.com)*.

POST

A postcard that is sent per airmail to any country in the world costs 70 ¥, airmail letters under 25 g 90 ¥. Branches are usually open Mon–Fri 9am–5pm, main post offices from 9am–7pm. Some main post offices are also open at the weekend.

PRICES & CURRENCY

Prices are generally very high, and can be compared with London or New York standards.

WEATHER IN TOKYO

	Jan	Feb	March	April	May	June	July	Aug	Sept	Oct	Nov	Dec
Daytime temperature in °C/°F	9/48	9/48	12/54	18/64	22/72	25/77	29/84	30/86	27/81	20/68	16/61	11/52
Night-time temperatures in °C/°F	-1/30	-1/30	3/37	4/39	13/55	19/66	22/72	23/73	19/66	13/55	7/45	1/34
☀ Sunshine hours/day	6	6	6	6	6	5	6	7	4	4	5	5
☂ Precipitation days/month	6	7	10	11	12	12	11	10	13	12	8	5

The currency in Japan is the yen (¥), which is also the smallest unit. Coins go up to 500 yen, notes start at 1000 yen.

PUBLIC TRANSPORT

In the cities, the colour-coded underground systems (signposted in English) are a help with orientation. It can be difficult to find the connection and buy the right ticket for commuter trains. If in doubt, ask the conductor, who will work out the correct fare for you for a small surcharge.

TIME

Japan is 9 hours ahead of Greenwich Mean Time (GMT), and 8 hours ahead during British summer time.

TIPPING

Tipping is not usual in restaurants or taxis or for porters.

TRAINS

The train is the ideal form of transport on almost any route. They are clean, safe and punctual, and the entry points are clearly identified on all the platforms. There are several train companies. On some routes, private trains are faster and more reasonable than the national network of Japan Rail (JR). Note that tickets are only valid for the issuing company. Purchase tickets for short journeys from a machine, but it's better to see a travel agent for long journeys. The *Japan Rail Pass* is recommended, which allows you to travel anywhere in the JR network (including JRS trains) for one, two or three weeks as often as you like. Outside Japan it is only available from Japan Travel Bureaus *(www.jrpass.com)*.

VAT

Consumption tax in Japan is 8 percent. It can usually be refunded in most normal shops or departments stores on presentation of a valid foreign passport. *www.taxfreeshops.jp*

WHERE TO STAY

Although reasonably-priced accommodation is available in Japan, it is not always to be recommended. Basic establishments (rooms less than 9000 yen) often do not meet Western standards. Tourists regularly complain about poor hygiene. The beds are futons, often with several people in a room. If breakfast is served, then it is a rice dish with cold fish, and usually only green tea; no coffee. It is also possible that foreigners are not welcome because of the language difficulties. Nor can it be assumed, sadly, that Japan's younger generation necessarily speaks any English. Business hotels are usually cramped and smoky, and women rarely seen there. Nor are the so-called "capsule hotels", usually near railway stations, recommended.

Strategically positioned, and often found off motorways near cities, are the highly imaginatively decorated or garishly illuminated establishments called "Love Hotels". Far from being brothels, they offer rooms by the hour for couples – including married couples – who want to escape the often confined circumstances at home. The hotels are not suitable for inexperienced tourists, but if you feel fairly safe in Japan they are a good place to spend a comfortable night, especially if you check in late at night, once the usual customers have gone home.

USEFUL PHRASES JAPANESE

PRONOUNCIATION

As an aid to pronunciation, the following phonetic spellings
have been used:
"o" for a short open vowel as in "hot"
"s" is a soft "s" as in "hiss"
"z" is voiced like the "z" in "buzz"
"h" after a vowel indicates that it is elongated
(like the elongation lines over the ō and ū at the front of the book)
"r" is not rolled, but is actually a combination of "r" and "l"
Double consonants (as in "chotto") have a short breath between the
two consonants (roughly tchot-!-to, jakkjoku roughly jak-!-kjoku)

AT A GLANCE

Yes./No./Maybe.	はい/いいえ/たぶん	[Hai./Ih-e./Tabun.]
Bitte./Danke.	どうぞ/ありがとう	[Dohzo./Arigatoh.]
Excuse me!	すみません	[Sumimasen!]
May I ...?	...してもいいですか	[... jitemo ih dess ka?]
Pardon?	すみません。もう一度お願いします	[Sumimasen. Moh ichido onegai shimass.]
I would like .../ Do you have ...?	...はありますか	[... wa arimass ka?]
How much is ...?	...はいくらですか	[...wa ikura dess ka?]
I (don't) like that.	...は気に入りました（入りません）	[...wa ki ni irimashita (irimasen).]
good/bad	良い/悪い	[joi/warui]
broken/not working	壊れています	[kowarete imass]
Help!/Careful!/Look out!	助けて/気をつけて/気をつけて	[Tasskete!/Ki o tsukete!/Ki o tsukete!]
Ambulance	救急車	[kyuhkyusha]
Police/Fire brigade	警察/消防	[keisatsu/schohboh]

HELLO & GOODBYE

Good morning!/Hello!	おはようございます/こんにちは	[Ohajoh gozaimass!/Konnichi-wa!]
Good evening!/ Good night!	こんばんは/お休みなさい	[Konban-wa!/Ojasuminasai!]

日本語が話せますか。

„Do you speak Japanese?" This guide will help you to say the basic words and phrases in Japanese.

Hello!/goodbye!	こんにちは/さようなら [Konnitschi-wa!/Sayohnara!]
Bye!	それじゃ、またね [Sore dja mata ne!]
My name is ...	...と申します [... to mohschimass.]
What is your name? (formal)	お名前を教えてください [Onama-e o oshiete kudasai?]
What's your name?	名前は何ですか [Nama-e wa nan dess ka?]
I'm from ...	...から来ました [... kara kimashita.]

DATE & TIME

Monday/Tuesday	月曜日/火曜日 [getsu-johbi/ka-johbi]
Wednesday/Thursday	水曜日/木曜日 [sui-johbi/moku-johbi]
Friday/Saturday	金曜日/土曜日 [kin-johbi/do-johbi]
Sunday/working day	日曜日/平日 [nichi-johbi/heichitsu]
Public holiday	祝日 [shuku-djitsu]
Today/tomorrow/yesterday	今日/明日/昨日 [kyoh/ashta/kinoh]
Hour/minute	時間/分 [djikan/fun]
Day/night/week	昼間/夜中 週間 [hiruma/jonaka/shuhkan]
Month/year	月/年 [getsu (gatsu)/nen]
What time is it?	今何時ですか [Ima nan-dshi dess ka?]
It's three o'clock.	三時です [San-dshi dess.]
It's half past three.	三時半です [San-dshi-han dess.]

OUT AND ABOUT

Open/closed	開いています/閉まっています [aite imass/shimatte imass]
Entrance/exit	入り口/出口 [irigutshi/degutshi]
Departure/arrival	出発/到着 [shuppatsu/tohshakku]
Toilets/Ladies/Gentlemen	お手洗い/女(性)/男(性) [ote-arai/dshosei/dansei]
Where is...?/Where are ...?	...はどこですか [...wa doko dess ka?]
Left/right	右/左 [migi/hidari]
Straight on/back	まっすぐ/戻る [massugu/modoru]
Near/far	近い/遠い [tshikai/toh-i]
Underground/taxi	地下鉄/タクシー [tshikatetsu/takshih]
Haltestelle/Taxistand	停/タクシー乗り場 [tei/takschih-noriba]
Town map/(country) map	地図 [tshizu]
Station/port	駅/港 [eki/minato]
Ariport	空港 [kuhkoh]
Timetable/ticket	時刻表/切符 [dshikokuhyoh/kippu]

FOOD & DRINK

Please reserve a table for four for us for this evening.	今夜の四人分の席を予約したいのですが [Konya no jonin-bun no seki o jojaku shitai no dess ka.]
Could we have the menu, please.	メニューをお願いします [Menjuh o onegai shimass.]
Please could I have ... ?	...を頂いてもいいですか [... o itadaite mo ih dess ka?]
Salt/pepper/sugar	塩/こしょう/砂糖 [shio/koshoh/satoh]
I would like to pay, please	お勘定お願いします [O-kandshoh onegai shimass.]
Bill/receipt	お勘定/領収書 [o-kandshoh/ljohshuhsho]

SHOPPING

Where is/are ...?	...はどこにありますか [...wa doko ni arimass ka?]
I would like .../I am looking for ...	...を探しています [... o sagashite imass.]
Chemist/drugstore	薬局/ドラッグストア [jakkjoku/doraggu-stoa]
Baker's/market	パン屋/市場 [pan-ja/itchiba]
Shopping centre/department store	ショッピングセンター/デパート [shopping sentah/depahto]
Supermarket	スーパー [suhpah]
Expensive/cheap/price	高い/安い/値段 [takai/jasui/nedan]

WHERE TO STAY

I have booked a room.	部屋を予約したのですが [Heja o jojaku shita no dess ga.]
Do you still have ...?	...はまだありますか [... wa mada arimass ka?]
Single room	シングルルーム [shinguru ruhm]
Double room	ダブルルーム [daburu ruhm]
Breakfast/half-board/full board	朝食付き/二食付き/三食付 [tshohshoku-tsuki/ni-shoku-tsuki/san-shoku-tsuki]
Shower/bath	シャワー/お風呂 [shawah/o-furo]
Key/room card	鍵/カードキー [kagi/kadoh-kih]
Baggage/suitcase/bag	荷物/スーツケース/かばん [nimotsu/suhtskehs/kaban]

BANKS & MONEY

Bank/cash machine	銀行/ＡＴＭ [ginkoh/Aej-Ti-Aem]
I would like to change ... Pound sterling/US-Dollar.	...ユーロを両替したいのですが [... pondo/amerikadoru o rjohga-e schitai no dess ga.]
Cash/ec card/credit card	現金/ヨーロッパのキャッシュカード/クレジットカード [genkin/johroppa no kyasshu-kahdo/kuredshitto-kahdo]

HEALTH

Doctor/dentist/paediatrician	医者/歯医者/小児科 [isha/ha-isha/shohnika]
Hospital/emergency practice	病院/当番医 [bjoh-in/tohban-i]
Temperature/pain	熱/痛み [netsu/itami]
Diarrhoea/nausea	下痢/吐き気 [geri/haki-ke]
Infected/injured	炎症があります/怪我をしました [enshoh ga arimass/kega o shimashita]
Plaster/bandage/painkillers/tablet	ばんそうこう/包帯/痛み止め/錠剤 [bansohkoh/hohtai/itami-dome/dshouzai]

TELECOMMUNICATIONS & MEDIA

Stamp/letter	切手/手紙 [kitte/tegami]
Postcard	葉書 [hagaki]
I would like a phone card for the fixed network.	固定電話用のテレフォンカード を下さい。 [Kotei-denwa joh no telefon-kahdo o kudasai.]
I'm looking for a prepaid card for my mobile.	携帯電話用のプリペイドカードを探しています [Keitai-denwa joh no puri-peido kahdo o sagaschite imass.]
Socket/adapter/charger	コンセント/アダプター/充電器 [konsento/adaputah/shudenki]
Computer/battery/rechargeable battery	コンピュータ/電池/充電池 [kompyuhta/denchi/judenchi]
Internet connection/WIFI	インターネット接続/無線LAN [intahnetto-setsuzoku/musen-lahn]
Email/file/print	メール/ファイルを印刷する [mehlu/failu/o insatsu suru]

NUMBERS

0	ゼロ [zero]	15	十五 [ju-go]
1	一 [ichi]	16	十六 [ju-roku]
2	二 [ni]	17	十七 [ju-shichi/juh-nana]
3	三 [san]	18	十八 [ju-hachi]
4	四 [shi, jon]	19	十九 [ju-kyuh/ju-ku]
5	五 [go]	70	七十 [nana-ju]
6	六 [roku]	80	八十 [hachi-ju]
7	七 [shichi, nana]	90	九十 [kyuh-ju]
8	八 [hachi]	100	百 [hyaku]
9	九 [kyu, ku]	200	二百 [nihyaku]
10	十 [ju]	1000	千 [sen]
11	十一 [ju-ichi]	2000	二千 [nisen]
12	十二 [ju-ni]	10,000	一万 [ichi-man]
13	十三 [ju-san]	1/2	二分の一 [ni-bun no ichi]
14	十四 [dju-shi ju-jon]	1/4	四分の一 [jon-bun no ichi]

ROAD ATLAS

The green line indicates the Discovery Tour "Japan at a glance"
The blue line indicates the other Discovery Tours

All tours are also marked on the pull-out map

Photo: Futarasan Shrine in Nikko

Exploring Japan

The map on the back cover shows how the area
has been sub-divided

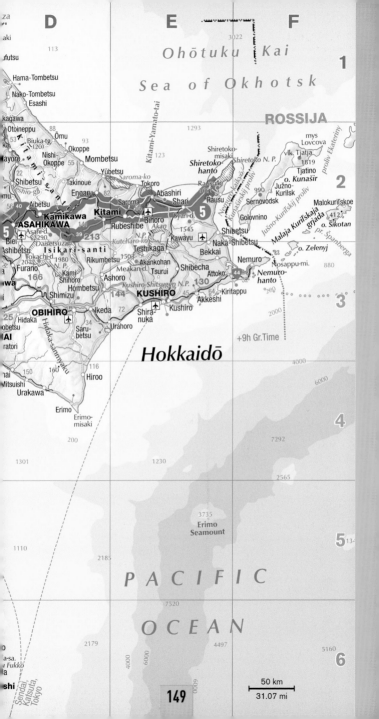

1

Nippon Kai

2000

Sea of Japan

1521

1298

Ū

120

Awashir

238

120

Hajiki-sa.

2 3063   *East Sea*

1873 Ryōtsu

M

Ar

Aikawa

Sado-shima

2103

✈ **NIIGATA**

Hegura-sh.

Sado Yahiko

Q.N.P.

Ogi Akadomari

Teradomari

Nii

Sa

58

Yamato

2000

Noto-hantō

Suzu-misaki

NAGAOKA

Wajima

Suzu

Kashiwazaki Ojiya

567

Noto-shima

Toyama-wan

JŌETSU

66

Togi Nanao

Asahi

Tōkamachi

Hakui

Itoigawa

3   **Himi**

Uozo

Myōkō

44

Arai

Miyama

124

Tsubata

TAKAOKA

TOYAMA

78 Tate-

122

Yoshino Tsu kogen

Zenpoku

Mikuni

1581

KANAZAWA

Tonami

3015

Chubu-

Suzaka

Numata

Mattō

✈   Ōmachi

NAGANO

KOMATSU

Suganuma

Hakusan

129

Shōmyō

Falls

UEDA

MAE-

BASHI

K

Kaga

N.P.

Kami-

oka

Hotaka-d.

18

103

25

Mikuni

107 Ogimachi

Kami-

oka

Taka-

yama

3190

Komoro

Tomioka

Silk Mill

TA

Hakus.

2702

Saku

MATSUMOTO

KU

G

FUKUI

189

Shiojiri

Chichibu

KAW

Ōno

224 41

Ontake-s.

Okaya

2895 Tama

TŌ

Takefu

51

Shiratori

3067

Matsu-

2899

195

Yamanashi

Kyogami-saki *Wakasa-wan*

Imajō

(1019)

101

Gero

Minami-

Shirane-s.

Chichibu

HACHIC

Amino

Wakasa-wan

Sekigahara

Neo

Q.N.P.

Q.N.P.

95

Nakatsu-

gawa

1192

2595

Otsuki

SA

Miyazu

Q.N.P.

Obama

Kino-

moto

Oto

Seki

Kiso-sanm.

KŌFU

Fujiyoshida

MIHA

ka

4 Amino

146

GIFU

Ena 162

157

Fuji-

Fuji-san

YOKO

Maizuru

139

Biwa-ko

Kani

Iida

N.P.

15

16

Fukuchiyama

Hikone

85

ICHI-

TAJIMI

Iida

52 Gotenba

FUJI

ODi

Kasuga

Tamba-

kochi

ŌGAKI

NOMIYA

NAGOYA

Honka-

wane

193

WAR

Ōmi-

Hachiman

1047

80

Naishi-sanm.

SHIMIZU

NUMAZU

10 11 12

KYŌTO

ŌTSU

YOKKAICHI

KARIYA

TOYOTA

OKAZAKI

SHIZUOKA

Izu-

hantō

92

TAKATSUKI

UJI

SUZUKA

107

ANJYO

TOYOKAWA

219

FUJIEDA

Shin

KOBE OSAKA

Hōryū-ji

HANDA

Kakegawa

Iro-sa.

SAKAI

NARA

HIGASHI-ŌS.

TSU

TOYOHASHI

HAMAMATSU

5   **KISHIWADA**

13

1 **MATSUZAKA**

Atsumi-

hantō

Omae-sa.

Enshū-nada

Suruga-wan

Misaki Gojyō

Q.N.P.

ISE

2

Toba

Shrines of Ise

Shikine-sh

Yoshino-

yama

246

Ago

Ise-shima N.P.

WAKAYAMA

Hakken-s.

Kii-Nagashima

171 *Kii-sanchi*

1915

Arida Q.N.P.

Kino-Gawa

Koya-san

Kumano-

nada

Gobō *Kumano*

4

Owase

Hongū

Q.N.P.

Kumano

Kumano

Kii-hantō

Tanabe Sanzan

1122

Shingū

Shirahama

✈

97 Katsuura

6   Shiono-mi.

42

Kushimoto

Naha, Naze

4000

153

150

2000

2000

AKITA
MORIOKA
Kakunodate
343
118
Omagari
1914
Miyako
Toda-sa.
Sanriku Fukko
Yamada
148
109
Yurihonjō
Hanamaki
Yokote
94
Nuzawa
144
Kitakami
Kamaishi
Chōkai Q.N.P.
2230
Chōkai-s.
13
138
Mizu-
sawa
1
KATA
52
Chūsonji
Jōfunato
1628
Ichinoseki
Kesennuma
UOKA
Shinjō
Kurikoma Q.N.P.
Hasama
84
112
Obana-zawa
77
200
148
Bandai-Asahi N.P.
Furu-
kawa
59
ISHINOMAKI
45
YAMAGATA
IZUMI
Shiogama
160
Tendō
SENDAI
Kinkasan-sh.
162
Nan-yō
88 1841
Zaō Zaō-s.
Ōsaki-Hachim-Shrine
Yonezawa
Q.N.P.
95
Iwanuma
2
ata
Iides.
Shiroishi
2105 Bandai-
13
2024
103
Kitakata Azuma-s.
Sōma
49
Nihon-matsu
FUKUSHIMA
Haramachi
AIZU-
WAKAMATSU
KŌRIYAMA
Namie
Sukagawa
1193
95
Tajima
6
Q.N.P.
Shira-
kawa
84
IWAKI
1915
164
Kuroiso
Yamatsuri
Kitaibaraki
Nikkō
Yaita
Fukuro
Falls
3
maichi
UTSU-
NOMIYA
105
HITACHI
SHI-
AGA
Mōka
80
KATSUTA
OYAMA
MITO
Shimo-
date
74
Koga
Ishioka
TSUCHIURA
Kasumigaura
Konosu
SAITAMA
Kashima
KASHIWA
Sawara
FUNABASHI
NARITA
Chōshi
CHIBA
Inubō-saki
KAWASAKI
Kujūkuri-
nada
FUJIS.
Mobara
KISARAZU
YOKOSUKA
Bōsō-hantō
Katsuura
Miura-
hantō
Q.N.P.
Tateyama
Nojima-sa.

PACIFIC

OCEAN

Japan Trench

50 km
151
31.07 mi

A 152

B Danjo-guntō

Kyūshū C

1
152
200
696
Uji-guntō

Ushibuka
Naga
Nagasaki
A
Kami-koshiki-sh.
Koshikishima-rettō
Sat
S
Shimo-Koshiki-sh.
Ku
Shimo-Koshiki
KA
Noma
Satsu
-ha
Ma
200

2
96
H i g a s h i   S h i n a   K a i
E a s t   C h i n a   S e a

Kusagaki-guntō
Kuro-sh
Kuchi
Erabu
Yaku-shir
Tokar

3
69
1213
1028

Nansei-shotō

Nakano-shima
979
Suwanose-shima
799
Akuseki-shima
Takara-shima
Tokara
Yokoate-shima
43

4
850
1074
229
N a n s e i - s h o t ō
Tori-shima
71

Kasari
Naze
68
694
80
Ō-shima
Setouchi
Kakeroma-shima
Tokuno-shima
645
Tokunoshima

5
1616
842
2000

Okinoerabu-shima
Wadomari
Amami-s
1678
S
ū

Iheya-shima
Izena-shima
Iheya
Yoron
Yoron-shima
Ie-shima
Oku
Motobu
61
58
498
Nago
131
Okinawa-shima

6
Kume-shima
790
Gushikawa
200
Aguni-shima
Keelung (Taiwan)
Kerama-rettō
NAHA
OKINAWA
Kin
Ishikawa
Gyokusendo
(Cave)
Okinawa-shotō
4000
6000
7881
Ryū
ū
R y ū k y ū - s h o t ō

154

Hitoyoshi
Ōkuchi
D
Saito
Takanabe
Kobayashi
156
Kirishima
Kirishima-y.
MIYAZAKI
Kinoshima
HIMA
Kokubo
MIYAKONOJŌ
Nichinan
Yaku N.P.
Shibushi
Kanoya
Shibushi
Nejime
806
2705
4944
1
Ibusuki
Sata
Ōsumi-hantō
Takeshima
Sata misaki
Nishi-no-Omote
Ōsumi-kaikyō
Tanega-shima
58
Kami-Yaku
Naka-Tane
Minami-Tane
4576
2
Miyanoura-d.
Yaku
Yaku-shima
Ōsumi-shotō
shima
138
289
4000
Ōsumi-shotō
5722
3486
4813
3
4000
4701
2268
4000
2484
4000
shima
6375
1985
4
2000
1436
6662
4000
6000
P A C I F I C
5
1678
6247
3781
O C E A N
3743
6
4000
Kita-daitō-shima
Minami-daitō-shima
Minami-Daitō

50 km
31.07 mi

4000

153
2000
2000
E
F
Ōsaka, Tōkyō

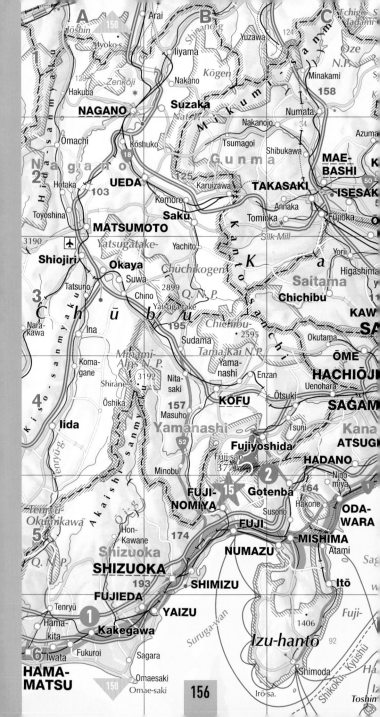

D | **E** | **F**

3

Nasu
Kuroiso
Shioya-Saki

Nikko N.P.
Kurobane
Yamatsuri
Kitaibaraki 1

Nikko
Yaita
Ōtawara
151
Takahagi

164
Fukuroda Falls

Falls
Imaichi
Daigo

Ashio
84
Kara-
suyama
Ibaraki

Ōya Kannon
Kawachi
Hitachiōta
HITACHI

Kanuma
UTSU-
Ichikai
2

NOMIYA

Mōka
Kasama
KATSUTA

Tochigi
Naka-
minato

ASHIKAGA
80

Sano
MITO

OYAMA
Shimodate

Tatebaya-
shi
Ishioka
74

Shimo-
KUMAGAYA
Koga
tsuma
100
Hokota

Kōnosu
Kuki
Ō
TSUCHIURA
0

Mitsukaido
Kasumiga-
Kitaura

KASUKABE
Toride
ura
Kashima

AGEO
NODA
Itako
3

OMIYA
URAWA
TŌKYŌ
Sawara

AMA
KASHIWA

NIIZA
ABIKO
NARITA

TUKO-
MATSUDO
Asashi
Chōshi

ROZAWA
ICHIKAWA
SAKURA
Inubō-saki

FUCHŪ
Tōkyō
FUNABASHI
Yokaichiba

ARA
CHIBA
Tōgane
4

YAMATO
Tōkyō-
ICHIHARA
Kujūkuri

KAWASAKI
Mobara
Kujūkuri-

wan
nada

YOKOHAMA
KISARAZU

Kamakura
Kimitsu
Chiba

Buddha
Ōhara

YOKOSUKA
352
Katsuura
5

UKA
Miura
Kamagova
Bōsō-hantō

Miura-
hanto
Minami-
Bōsō

Tateyama
Q.N.P.
2000

Nojima-saki

Izu-Ōshima

shima
Miyaki-shima

25 km
6

P. Niijima
15.54 mi

151

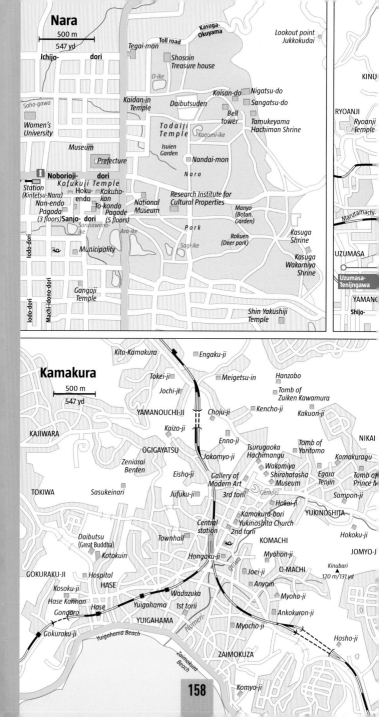

Nara

500 m
547 yd

Ichijo- dori

Saho-gawa

Women's
University

Tegai-mon

Toll road

Kasuga-
Okuyama

Lookout point
Jukkokudai

Shosoin
Treasure house

O-ike

Kaidan-in
Temple

Daibutsuden

Kaisan-do

Nigatsu-do

Sangatsu-do

Bell
tower

Tamukeyama
Hachiman Shrine

Todaiji
Temple

Kagami-ike

Museum

Prefecture

Isuien
Garden

Nandai-mon

Nara

Noborioji- dori
Kofukuji Temple
Station Hoku- Kokuho-
(Kintetsu-Nara) endo kan
Nan-endo To-kondo
Pagoda (5 floors)
(3 floors) Sanjo- dori

Sarusawano-
ike

National
Museum

Research Institute for
Cultural Properties

Manyo
(Botan.
Garden)

Kasuga
Shrine

Iodo-dori

Ara-ike

Municipality

Sagi-ike

Park

Rokuen
(Deer park)

Kasuga
Wakamiya
Shrine

Machi-idono-dori
Iodo-dori

Gangoji
Temple

Shin Yakushiji
Temple

KINU

RYOANJI

Ryoanji
Temple

Marutamachi-

UZUMASA

Uzumasa-
Tenjngawa

YAMANO

Shijo-

Kamakura

500 m
547 yd

Kita-Kamakura

Engaku-ji

KAJIWARA

Tokei-ji

Jochi-ji

Meigetsu-in

Hanzobo

Tomb of
Zuiken Kawamura

YAMANOUCHI-JI

Choju-ji

Kencho-ji

Kakuon-ji

Kaizo-ji

OGIGAYATSU

Enno-ji

Jokomyo-ji

Tsurugaoka
Hachimangu

Tomb of
Yoritomo

NIKAI

Zeniarai
Benten

Eisho-ji

Wakamiya
Shirahatasha
Museum

Kamakuragu

TOKIWA

Sasukeinari

Gallery of
Modern Art
3rd torii

Egara
Tenjin

Tomb of
Prince M

Jufuku-ji

Gempei

Sampon-ji

Hokai-ji

YUKINOSHITA

Central
station

Kamakura-bori
Yukinoshita Church
2nd torii

Daibutsu
(Great Buddha)

Townhall

KOMACHI

Hokoku-ji

Kotokuin

Hongaku-ji

Myohon-ji

JOMYO-J

GOKURAKU-JI

Hospital
HASE

Joei-ji

O-MACHI

Kosoku-ji

Kinubari
120 m/131 yd

Hase Kannon
Gongoro

Hase

Wadazuka
1st torii

Anyoin

Myoho-ji

Yuigahama

Gokuraku-ji

Yuigahama Beach

YUIGAHAMA

Ankokuron-ji

Myocho-ji

Hosho-ji

Nameri

Zaimokuza
Beach

ZAIMOKUZA

Komyo-ji

158

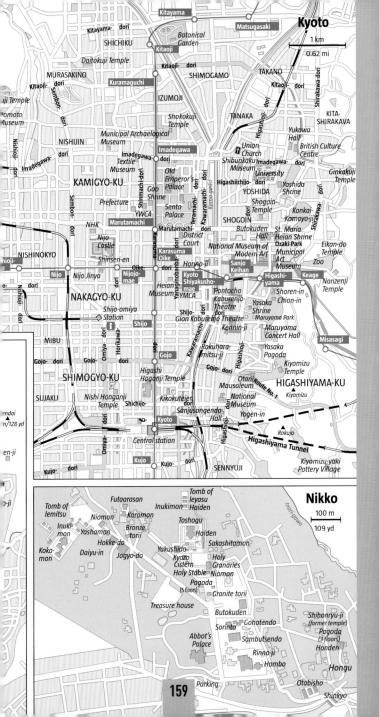

Osaka

KITA-KU

Umeda Sky Building

Hattori Park

Expo Memorial Park

Tenjinbashi-suji

Tenjinbashi

Kyoto

Miyakojima

Panasonic Center

Nakazakicho

Osaka Station

Umeda Koma Theatre

Ogimachi Park

Ogimachi

Yodo gawa

Umeda

UMEDA

MIYAKOJIMA-KU

Sankei-Kaikan

Osaka Maru Building

Minami-Morimachi

Temmangu Shrine

Shopping street

Sakuranomiya Park

Fujita Art Museum

Japan Mint

Neya gawa

Hirano gawa

University Hospital

Mainichi Building

Court of Justice

Dojima gawa

Central market

Festival building

Town Hall

Library

Museum of Oriental Ceramics

Japan Mint

International trade centre

Bank of Japan

Nakanoshima Park

Okawa

School of Dentistry Osaka University

Tosabori gawa

Tosabori-dori

Higobashi

Kitahama

Stock Exchange

Temmabashi

Park

Castle

CHUOKU

Kita mido Temple

Chamber of Industry and Commerce

Prefecture

Police Headquarters

Osaka Museum of History

Hokoku Shrine

Technical Centre

Utsubo Park

Hommachi-dori

Hommachi

Chuo-O-dori

Sakaisuji-hommachi

N.H.K.

Tanimachi Yon-chome

Ruins of Naniwa-no-miya

Awaza

Modern Transportation Museum

Universal Studios

Kosei Nenkin Building

Minami-mido Temple

Kozugu Shrine

Hospital

Nissei Baseball Stadium

Christian Centre

Nishiohashi

Shinsaibashi

Matsuyamachi

Nishi-Nagahori

Yotsubashi

Nagahori-bashi

Ikutama Shrine

Tanimachi Roku-chome

Nagahori-dori

Sanadayama Park

Central Library

NISHI-KU

Dotonburigawa

MINAMI-KU

Naniwa-suji

Yotsubashi-suji

Shinsaibashi-suji

Midosuji

Matsuyamachi-suji

Uemachi-suji

Sakuragawa

Namba Station

Dotonbori-dori

Asahi-za-Theatre

Nipponbashi

Tanimachi Kyu-chome

NANIWA-KU

Namba

Shin-Kabuki-za-Theatre

National Bunraku Theatre

Sennichimae-dori

Kintetsu

Tsuruhashi

NAMBA

Ebisubashi-suji

Sakai-suji

TENNOJI-KU

Crafts Museum

Daikokucho

Imamiya Ebisu Shrine

Ebisucho

Shitennoji Temple

Tsutenkaku Tower

Tennoji Park

Zoo

SHIN-SEKAI

Spa World

Library

Art Museum

College of Education

NISHI-NARI-KU

Botan Garden

Bureau

Tennoji Station

Dobutsuen-Mae

Municipal University (Medical Faculty)

Abeno

Abeno Haurkas

Osaka

500 m
547 yd

Tengachaya

ABENO-KU

Sumiyoshi Shrine
Wakayama
Kansai Airport

160

Nagai Park,
Museum of Natural History,
University

Harbour, exhibition grounds

Autobahn, mehrspurige Straße – in Bau Highway, multilane divided road – under construction		Autoroute, route à plusieurs voies-en construction Autosnelweg, weg met meer rijstroken – in aanleg
Fernverkehrsstraße – in Bau Trunk road – under construction		Route à grande circulation – en construction Weg voor interlokaal verkeer – in aanleg
Hauptstraße Principal highway		Route principale Hoofdweg
Nebenstraße Secondary road		Route secondaire Overige verharde wegen
Fahrweg, Piste Practicable road, track		Chemin carrossable, piste Weg, piste
Straßennummerierung Road numbering	E20 11 70 26 5 40 9	Numérotage des routes Wegnummering
Entfernungen in Kilometer Distances in kilometers	259 130 129	Distances en kilomètres Afstand in kilometers
Höhe in Meter – Pass Height in meters – Pass	1365	Altitude en mètres – Col Hoogte in meters – Pas
Eisenbahn – Eisenbahnfähre Railway – Railway ferry		Chemin de fer – Ferry-boat Spoorweg – Spoorpont
Autofähre – Schifffahrtslinie Car ferry – Shipping route		Bac autos – Ligne maritime Autoveer – Scheepvaartlijn
Wichtiger internationaler Flughafen – Flughafen Major international airport – Airport	✈ ✈	Aéroport importante international – Aéroport Belangrijke internationale luchthaven – Luchthaven
Internationale Grenze – Provinzgrenze International boundary – Province boundary		Frontière internationale – Limite de Province Internationale grens – Provinciale grens
Unbestimmte Grenze Undefined boundary		Frontière d'Etat non définie Rijksgrens onbepaalt
Zeitzonengrenze Time zone boundary	-4h Greenwich Time -3h Greenwich Time	Limite de fuseau horaire Tijdzone-grens
Hauptstadt eines souveränen Staates National capital	**MANILA**	Capitale nationale Hoofdstad van een souvereine staat
Hauptstadt eines Bundesstaates Federal capital	**Kuching**	Capitale d'un état fédéral Hoofdstad van een deelstat
Sperrgebiet Restricted area		Zone interdite Verboden gebied
Nationalpark National park		Parc national Nationaal park
Antikes Baudenkmal Ancient monument	∴	Monument antiques Antiek monument
Sehenswertes Kulturdenkmal Interesting cultural monument	✶ Angkor Wat	Monument culturel interéssant Bezienswaardig cultuurmonument
Sehenswertes Naturdenkmal Interesting natural monument	✶ Ha Long Bay	Monument naturel interéssant Bezienswaardig natuurmonument
Brunnen Well		Puits Bron
MARCO POLO Erlebnistour 1 MARCO POLO Discovery Tour 1		MARCO POLO Tour d'aventure 1 MARCO POLO Avontuurlijke Routes 1
MARCO POLO Erlebnistouren MARCO POLO Discovery Tours		MARCO POLO Tours d'aventure MARCO POLO Avontuurlijke Routes
MARCO POLO Highlight	⭐	MARCO POLO Highlight

INDEX

This index contains all of the towns and cities, destinations and some of the main terms used in this travel guide. Bold page numbers refer to the main entry.

CREDITS

WRITE TO US

e-mail: info@marcopologuides.co.uk

Did you have a great holiday?
Is there sor
Whatever i
Whether yo
to errors or
MARCO PO
from you.
We do ever
very latest

Nevertheless, despite all of our authors'
thorough research, errors can creep
LO does not accept any
s. Please contact us by

Travel Publishing Ltd
ineham Business Park
e, Chineham
Hampshire RG24 8AL
m

PICTURE CRED
Cover Photogr
Photos: Corbis: berg (90); Getty Images: P. A. Asikai-
nen (126/127),   (87), A. Spatari (131), T. Tontinikorn
(78/79); Getty   (22); huber-images: T. Draper (72),
L. Grandadam   /PictureFinders (1 top); R. Köhler
(flap right, 6, 4   2, 64), M. Kirchgessner (26/27, 28
left, 30/31), F. Molères (102), Ch. Papsch (61), J.-B. Rabouan (119), J. F. Raga (14), J. Souteyrat (57); Laif/Arcaid:
B. Simmons (40/41); Laif/hemis.fr: F. Guiziou (7, 31, 93, 135), D. Zylberyng (4 below, 76); Laif/Polaris: D. Tacon
(19 below); Laif/Redux/NYT: K. Sasaki (18 below); Laif/Redux/VWPics: L. Vallecillos (84); Laif/robertharding:
Ch. Kober (146/147); Look/age fotostock (48); Look/Design Pics (108); Look/robertharding (52); mauritius images: J. F. Raga (54, 68, 75, 100/101, 134 top), A. Tanner (71), S. Vidler (flap left, 63, 95, 96, 112/113, 134 below),
J. Warurton-Lee (2, 5, 66/67); mauritius images/age: (12/13, 51, 58, 89, 115), L. Vallecillos (37); mauritius
images/Alamy: (10, I. Masterton (20/21), U. Switucha (39); mauritius images/Diversion: (32/33, 105, 110/111,
124/125), S. Kato (34); mauritius images/foodcollection (18 centre); mauritius images/imagebroker: O. Mak-
symenko (4 top, 17); mauritius images/Photononstop (30); mauritius images/robertharding: S. Black (47);
picture-alliance: Kyodo (98); picture-alliance/dpa: A. Sato (19 top), M. Taga (25); H. Pohling (9, 132, 132/133);
P. Spierenburg (11); varioimages/RHPL (8)

1st edition 2018
Worldwide Distribution: Marco Polo Travel Publishing Ltd, Pinewood, Chineham Business Park, Crockford Lane,
Basingstoke, Hampshire RG24 8AL, United Kingdom. Email: sales@marcopolouk.com
© MAIRDUMONT GmbH & Co. KG, Ostfildern
Chief editor: Marion Zorn
Authors: Angela Köhler, Rainer Köhler; editor: Karin Liebe
Programme supervision: Susanne Heimburger, Tamara Hub, Nikolai Michaelis, Kristin Schimpf, Martin Silbermann
Picture editor: Gabriele Forst, Anja Schlatterer; What's hot: wunder media, München
Cartography road atlas: © MAIRDUMONT, Ostfildern; Cartography pull-out map: © MAIRDUMONT, Ostfildern
Cover design, p. 1, pull-out map cover: Karl Anders – Büro für Visual Stories, Hamburg;
design inside: milchhof:atelier, Berlin; design p. 2/3, discovery tours: Susan Chaaban Dipl.-Des. (FH)
Translated from German by Mo Croasdale
Editorial office: SAW Communications, Redaktionsbüro Dr. Sabine A. Werner, Mainz: Julia Gilcher, Marc Niemeyer,
Cosima Talhouni, Dr. Sabine A. Werner; Prepress: SAW Communications, Mainz, in cooperation with
alles mit Medien, Mainz
Phrase book in cooperation with Ernst Klett Sprachen GmbH, Stuttgart,
Editorial by PONS Wörterbücher
All rights reserved. No part of this book may be reproduced, stored in a
retrieval system or transmitted in any form or by any means (electronic,
mechanical, photocopying, recording or otherwise) without prior written
permission from the publisher.
Printed in China

MIX
Paper from
responsible sources
FSC® C124385

DOS & DON'TS 👆

Avoid disharmony at all costs – and don't wear your loo slippers

SHAKING HANDS

People will greet you with bows when you enter a hotel, restaurant or shop. In the provinces in particular, the Japanese will be disconcerted if you try to shake hands with them. You (as a foreigner) don't have to bow. A friendly face will suffice.

DON'T FORGET TO TAKE YOUR SHOES OFF

If you are staying in a Japanese guesthouse, visiting a restaurant with straw mats on the floor or looking at a temple or shrine, you'll have to take your shoes off. The Japanese prefer to wear slippers on these occasions. One particularly tricky area is toilets in shoe-free areas. Special slippers are provided there, for obvious reasons. Time and again, though, foreigners forget to change into their house slippers when they have finished their business, and end up strolling around the site in their loo slippers – much to the amusement of the Japanese.

IGNORE THE TAXI RULES

Rule no. 1: Never touch a door. The driver will open and close the back door from his seat. You will be considered a hick for not knowing this. Passengers usually sit in the back. Apart from a few exceptions, taxi drivers speak no other languages, including English. Remember to give them your destination in Japanese.

WASH BEFORE COMMUNAL BATHING

Foreigners are almost always regarded with disdain when relaxing in the wonderful hot springs (*onsen*). The Japanese worry that the *gaijin* enter the communal bath without washing first. You must first scrub and soap yourself thoroughly – so that everyone can see. The Japanese usually squat on wooden stools, and pour water over themselves from a little wooden tub. Use lots of soap to convince them!

TRAVEL AT THE WRONG TIME

Even the Japanese complain about the heat in July and August. It's a little cooler in early summer, from mid-May to June, but very rainy. Late summer with its hurricanes is also usually wet and not very inviting. Spring and autumn are lovely, but avoid the Golden Week from the end of April/early May, because half Japan is out and about over this chain of public holidays. The same applies to *O-Bon* in the middle of August.

ARGUING

The Japanese have a marked aversion to open confrontation and a strong desire for harmony, which is often more highly regarded than the truth. Suppress your personal feelings. The Japanese believe that emotions should only be felt. It is considered indelicate to express them verbally or to show them.